THE 24 HOUR WOMAN

Advance Acclaim for
THE 24 HOUR WOMAN
How High Achieving, Stressed Women Manage It All and Still Find HAPPINESS

"This book is really easy to read, with examples leading to learning points delivered in point forms that make it simple to remember and digest. Something in particular rang with me when I read the book: the continuous call for action that really makes you want to step up! I like the confidence booster — feel the fear, but do it anyway. The book is a practical guide for any woman who wishes to take her life into her own hands, in simple, conversational English. You will be left asking questions about your own life and the legacy you want to leave behind. For those looking for affirmative examples to step out of their comfort zones — read the book!"

— Low Chin Loo, President,
Financial Women's Association Singapore (2012-2015)

"*The 24-Hour Woman* allows us the opportunity to 'pull back the curtains to a vibrant and joyous life' learning to use the technology and resources, which at one time may have overwhelmed us, to instead find balance and fulfillment. Remember, the journey is where we are on the road. What's important to you? This book will help you enjoy the journey while focusing on your end-goal, finding the joy you desire while relentlessly heading, each of us, toward our own legacy."

— Lori Ruff, CEO, Integrated Alliances,
Forbes Top 10 Social Media Power Influencer Woman

"Practical AND Profound advice to keep the legacy (big picture) in mind, while juggling all the minute details that take up a woman's 24 hours."

— Mrs. Laura Hwang, President
Singapore Council for Women (2000-2014)

"Every woman who thinks she has her life balanced should read this book. I thought I had it all covered. Reading this book opened my eyes to how I can have an even better, happier, less stressful life with just a few small changes."

— **Laura Steward, CEO** Wisdom Learned, LLC, Award Winning Best-Selling Author of *What Would a Wise Woman Do?*, International Speaker and Caregiver

"We can have it all, on our own terms, at our own pace and by our own definition of what a good life is. Live well, have a family, work smart, and feel good — this book captures the empowering spirit of translating opportunities into possibilities."

— **Claire Chiang**, Chairperson, Employer Alliance, a network of organizations tasked to promote work flexibility and smart workplaces

"In *The 24 Hour Woman*, Cheryl Liew-Chng takes a comprehensive look at why working women feel stressed and overwhelmed, and what they can do about it. Carve some time out of your 24-hour day to read it!"

— **Carol Fishman Cohen**, Co-founder, iRelaunch, Co-author, *Back on the Career Track*

"Cheryl's passion and enthusiasm comes through in every page of this remarkable book, chock full with practical tips and pointers for every woman — first, the timely (and insistent!) reminder to identify what matters most to her, and then bringing her along the journey to turn this aspiration into reality. Truly, a *read most excellent!*"

— **Jennifer Lee, M.D.**, Chairperson of Agency for Integrative Care and Former CEO of KK Women's and Children's Hospital

"*The 24-Hour Woman* shows a very accurate analysis of the current changes in modern women's lives, which are offering new opportunities for development, but at the same time creating a new set of challenges. The book offers practical suggestions on how to deal with those challenges. This book is a must-read for women wanting to be successful in life in this modern age."

— **Jose Gomez, M.D.**, Board Certified Psychiatrist, Ex-Director of a Medical School at INTEC. Founding Fellow of the Institute for Coaching, Harvard University, School of Medicine

"This book is for women who are on the go. This book is for men, too. Pushing beyond the bounds of a single day, Cheryl challenges myths and gives homework in the form of strategies to put into practice. Scenarios and myths are explored as interviews with real 24-hour women heroes are offered as examples of what works. This is your guide to reinventing your peace and productivity from the inside out. Your habits will be challenged and you will create a different blueprint for your day. Follow Cheryl Liew-Chng's advice and roadmap and you will enjoy the benefits of a little more sanity to what seems constantly to be a chaotic world.

— **Dr Wayne D Pernell**, Best-Selling Author and Hay House Featured Author, High Performance Leadership Coach

THE 24 HOUR WOMAN

*How High Achieving, Stressed Women
Manage It All and Still Find* HAPPINESS

CHERYL LIEW-CHNG

NEW YORK

THE 24 HOUR WOMAN
How High Achieving, Stressed Women Manage It All and Still Find HAPPINESS

© 2015 CHERYL LIEW-CHNG.

Published in New York, New York, by Morgan James Publishing. Morgan James and The Entrepreneurial Publisher are trademarks of Morgan James, LLC. www.MorganJamesPublishing.com

The Morgan James Speakers Group can bring authors to your live event. For more information or to book an event visit The Morgan James Speakers Group at www.TheMorganJamesSpeakersGroup.com.

A **free** eBook edition is available with the purchase of this print book.

CLEARLY PRINT YOUR NAME ABOVE IN UPPER CASE

Instructions to claim your free eBook edition:
1. Download the BitLit app for Android or iOS
2. Write your name in **UPPER CASE** on the line
3. Use the BitLit app to submit a photo
4. Download your eBook to any device

ISBN 978-1-63047-237-5 paperback
ISBN 978-1-63047-238-2 eBook
Library of Congress Control Number:
2014937703

Cover Design by:
Rachel Lopez
www.r2cdesign.com

Interior Design by:
Bonnie Bushman
bonnie@caboodlegraphics.com

In an effort to support local communities, raise awareness and funds, Morgan James Publishing donates a percentage of all book sales for the life of each book to Habitat for Humanity Peninsula and Greater Williamsburg.

Get involved today, visit
www.MorganJamesBuilds.com

Habitat
for Humanity®
Peninsula and
Greater Williamsburg
Building Partner

DEDICATION

This book is lovingly dedicated to
the many 24-Hour Women I have been blessed to meet
who have walked the path, found fulfillment and
happiness, and shown me the way.

"Many daughters have done virtuously
but thou excellest them all."
—Proverbs 31:29 KJV

CONTENTS

Introduction

THE PREMISE

Each of us has twenty-four hours in a single day; why is it that some women find *success, happiness,* and *fulfillment* in their days—while others discover only *frustration* and *fatigue*?

For the past ten years, I've worked globally with women in the areas of career development and work-life challenges. My goal and passion lie in helping them *live more vibrant and joyful lives.*

Throughout my work, I quickly recognized a trend; one of the most frequently asked questions I've heard is: "We all have twenty-four hours in a day: so how do we *do it all?*"

My question back to those women today is: *"Do we really need to do it all?"* My response came after much reflection. You see, I found myself tackling the question of "how to do it all" so frequently that I developed my own response based on what I found works—and doesn't work—for women worldwide.

Eventually, someone told me, "Cheryl, you've been doing so much and are spending so much time with us, helping us with this issue; we know a lot of other people out there who need the same message." That got me thinking, two years ago, about how I could reach out to more women who are obviously experiencing the same challenge of managing a mere twenty-four hours each day.

At the end of the day, as women look across the fence and see some who are more happy and fulfilled than others, I discovered that the universal question women want to know is: *how can we have the same for ourselves?* That question, and the conversation that preceded it, gave birth to *The 24-Hour Woman* as a book.

We live in a highly mobile, always on, 24/7 society. Our modern, hectic, and sometimes chaotic environment forces us to commit to more, thus squeezing more out of each day. Whether you are a working mom coping with kids and a career, a caregiver juggling between the needs of a dependent and your work, a thriving and multi-talented entrepreneur taking on the world, or a baby boomer lacking the possibility of true "retirement," this book is for you—offering a tool for building the beautiful tapestry of your legacy, even amidst the challenges of your hectic and sometimes chaotic life.

Why now? With career opportunities abounding in business, and our culture and society transforming in the last decade, now is the opportune time to pull back the curtains to unveil a vibrant and joyous life. Technology (new social media and collaborative systems that allow telecommuting and flexible work), demographic shifts (gender and generation shifts that increase the number of women in the workplace as the population ages), and globalization (the world feeling a lot smaller than it once did) have changed the context of business and the workplace. These shifts provide new options for women to plug in, literally, to new careers and work setups—locally, regionally, and internationally.

At some point, as women attempt to juggle all of their expectations, they often get struck by the realization that they need to be more authentic to themselves, so that they can have lives that are more vibrant and happy. As you can see, all of these common themes—although they are common—also have the tendency to pull us in conflicting directions. That's where the tension of the 24-Hour Woman comes in. *We all have twenty-four hours. What do we choose to do with them? Do we focus on what is right in front of us? Or do we dare to look further out at the horizon of twenty-four hours—and what might be beyond it?* Certainly, our day-to-day habits matter. But what I want to encourage you to do proactively now—because I think at some point in your life you will be *compelled* to ask yourself some of these same questions—is to look at the longer-term view, which is the horizon, or your legacy.

As long as you keep your legacy in perspective, even if life throws you lemons and disrupts your plan, you will know that you are working towards a bigger picture. You can learn to adapt and evolve with resilience.

As a 24-Hour Woman, you will find yourself *on the path* of continuous growth and development—and *in the process* of creating. As life shows up, or as you move into different stages in life, the themes might be the same, but the way that you evolve and handle them will be different. What will remain the same is your objective of living a more vibrant and joyful life.

The 24-Hour Woman is one who recognizes her challenges and is equipped to enjoy her work-life-play optimally, taking into consideration her own well-being, as well as the well-being of those with whom she is in relationship. This could include children, a spouse, extended family, coworkers, a boss, clients, and more. The 24-Hour Woman is no longer daunted by the challenges around her, but instead inspired by them—because she is equipping herself with time-tested and cutting-edge strategies and tools, embracing the right attitudes, and creating her own success of joy and vibrancy as she journeys towards her life destiny.

The 24-Hour Woman is "STRESSED" like the rest of women, having a thousand tasks on her to-do list, but she is mindful that **managing it all doesn't mean having it all. Instead, it means that she can navigate life successfully by focusing first on the legacy she wants to build. The 24-Hour Woman is high achieving on her own terms—and not steered by success as defined by society or the media. She knows what's important to her and sets her heart on it.**

This book is divided into three distinct parts:

Part 1: The Opportunity and Myths of "Having It All"

Like no other time in history, diverse and fulfilling opportunities abound for women both at the workplace and in starting their own businesses. The challenge of managing "all" of life, regardless of whether single or married, with dependents or without, however, is still perpetual. In Part I, The 24-Hour Woman will assess her current state within her environment and learn: *What's your opportunity now? What is holding you back?*

Part II: The Pillars of the Vibrant 24-Hour Woman

Part II unveils and applies the five Pillars of the 24-Hour Woman, which become core to the book's philosophy. Each Pillar is set in dynamic interplay with the seven core areas of life: *family, relationships, health, career/business, recreation, finance, and spirituality.* In this context, these five Pillars are put into play on a daily basis.

Peppered with actionable how-tos, specific sections will be devoted to each of these Pillars, while drawing applications to the seven core areas of life. Case studies of others who have "walked the talk" will encourage the 24-Hour Woman to take action. Strategies and tools wrap up the sections with questions that will encourage her to journal her journey.

Part III: The Revolution is On

In addition to providing further nurturing opportunities for the 24-Hour Woman to practice the Pillars, Part III also provides wisdom on how to avoid potential problems. The 24-Hour Woman will be given the heads-up to potential issues; she will also be given the skills for success in navigating them. She will learn to *fear not for what's ahead*, as she will have created her own roadmap. Finally, she will be able to bring together all of the concepts in the book to reach towards a greater goal. She'll be ready to thrive with vibrancy and joy again—as she builds her life LEGACY as a 24-Hour Woman. It's time for a change that will impact not only the moment, but the future as well; the revolution is on!

By the time the 24-Hour Woman has completed this portion of the book, she will be ready to pay it forward and recruit others to join this positive, joyful movement.

Are you ready to be a 24-Hour Woman?

How to Use This Book

I highly recommend that you journal your way through the book. Each chapter offers strategies, tactics, and stories—and specific sections that will allow you to work through specific areas of life. Keep an open mind, go through the process, and allow yourself to dream and create again—unfolding the vibrant life that you so desire. *Only you* can design and make these transitions. Journaling helps to keep you focused on discoveries about yourself, and helps you to keep track of your milestones of *awesomeness*.

In addition to the main content, there are specific segments that call for your review and action. Don't worry about how you will get through them, and don't be overwhelmed. Work through the process just like many of my students (and I!) have done. You will find that the process is well worth it!

Putting It Into Practice. In each of these sections, we focus on a frequently asked question from The 24-Hour Women Community.

Taking It Home. This portion highlights strategies for tackling issues that arise at home.

The 24-Hour Woman Speaks. Think you are struggling alone? Think again. Learn from other women—their challenges and how they creatively and resolutely work around issues. This section includes interviews from diverse women around the globe and allows us to learn from them while also engaging with our community. Links are included to view longer versions of the interviews online.

The 24-Hour Woman Signpost. As we conclude each chapter, you will see this section called The 24-Hour Signpost. This is where the chapter discussion becomes focused on YOU. I strongly encourage you to use this section to feed your journal entries. As you start a journal (or continue one that you already have), spend adequate time reflecting and answering the questions in each 24-Hour Woman Signpost section. Doing so will benefit you greatly—enabling you to step back from the hustle and bustle and find yourself again.

If you are meeting as a group, these book features will help facilitate discussions and creative solutions to be explored as a community. (For more resources for group meetings, please visit The24HourWoman. com/Resources)

This book is very exciting to me. I really love what I do, but I've also come to the realization that not all of us are at that place of blessing—loving what we do. When I look across the range of women I've worked with or encountered, I've seen very successful women who say, "I have to make this choice to do such and such, because the other option of living a life that is more true to my desires is not possible," and they're unhappy about it. The thing is, if we consciously design our lives and become aware of where we are and how we want to move—starting from a position of appreciation and gratitude for what we already have—we will have a much more joyful journey. We will be fulfilled on a daily basis, rather than just waiting for the big day when we finally will have arrived.

My excitement is not just over the book, but also over my global work with women in this area of thriving in a 24/7 world. I love seeing the transformation, the difference, the joy that is radiated from their faces when I meet them in their journeys; that is priceless.

Living a life that is vibrant and joyful builds our legacy: a life that is *most excellent*. Are you ready? Read on!

Chapter 1

THE OPPORTUNITY

"Seize the day."
–from the movie, **"Dead Poets Society"**

*C*ome, and meet some friends of mine. Each is intelligent, confident, and high achieving in her own right. Do you know anyone like them? Are you asking questions like theirs?

Meet Esther: a Gen Xer Who Cares for Dependents, Has a Full-time Career, and Is Both Work and Family Focused

Esther is the youngest employee ever in the history of her international engineering firm to have been appointed operations director. She has a bright career future before her at the age of thirty-two.

Esther and her husband, Daniel, are raising their young son, Mack, who spends much of his day with a caregiver. Esther and Daniel spend their weekends with Mack, who is their only child.

Esther has a wonderful marriage and loves her work. Her life looks rosy indeed to outside observers. Unknown to others, however, is that Esther has a second baby on the way. Now, at the start of her first trimester, she wonders how she can break this news to her supervisor without impacting her own future career opportunities. She knows that, in order to advance to the next level in her career, she will be expected to be mobile. She understands that this mobility might include working for a period of time in another country or taking on roles that would require frequent global travel. As it stands, she manages a team of five who are diverse in terms of culture, gender, and generation. The team is also diverse geographically, so she manages them both physically—in the same location where she is—and virtually. Needless to say, Esther has to spend a lot of time resolving complex conflicts and dealing with the diverse expectations of her team.

Esther knows that quitting is not an option, as Daniel and she need a dual income to maintain their current standard of living. But she is conflicted and overwhelmed. She already feels guilty and stressed each time she needs to take calls from home or hold meetings on weekends. The ultimate emotional blow to Esther happened when Mack fell the other day, and he ran into the arms of his caregiver instead of to Esther—who was standing right beside him. It broke her heart and left her wondering, *what can I do to live a life where I excel at work AND in my family life?*

Meet Jen: a Baby Boomer Retiree
Who Works, with Children Away from Home

Jen has an impeccable work ethic. The one and only company she has worked in for in thirty years is the same one she wants to continue working for until retirement. She has just discovered, however, that retirement may not happen when she'd originally expected. Jen has learned that she will need to continue working to fund her ongoing needs. The thought of continuing to work at this pace sends shivers down her back. She had thought that she could finally slow down and smell the roses, as her health is not as good as it once was.

To make matters worse, her current boss is the same age as her son. In recent months, she has had run-ins with her boss with regards to showing respect and recognition of her contributions. Having been in the same workplace for the last thirty years, she is not sure if she can start over in the "whole new world" out there. However, being fiercely independent, she loathes asking her grown-up children for support. She wants to explore her work options and improve her relationship with her boss. *How can I live a more vibrant and fulfilling life? Isn't this really what life is all about?* she asks herself daily.

Meet Sylvia: a Gen Y, Career-Focused Woman, Who Also Wants to Have Some Fun in Life

Yet to relinquish her fight to retain a life outside of work, Sylvia is every bit of the young, enthusiastic millennial—eager to prove herself and live life by her own rules. She recently asked her supervisor, "Why do we have to go to work at the same time every day, and to the same place? The commute to work is terrible. I am more productive working from home or somewhere more informal. After all, my work can be done entirely from my laptop!" Sylvia was amazed with her supervisor's answer that *it has always been this way*, and that she should adapt if she wants to be promoted and advance in her career.

Now, she needs to show that she is present and active at work. She has learned how to work "smart." But she is realizing she should not be so efficient, because it does not pay to get things done quickly. She will still have to hang around the office until the clock strikes quitting time and she and the zillions of others in the office leave for home.

Sighing, she wishes she could go join the master ceramics class of a famous potter who is in town just for the season. Alas, the class is in the late afternoon, and there is no way she can leave early to pursue her passion.

Meet Abigail: an Entrepreneur Who Thought Running Her Own Business Would Give Her More Free Time to Do What She Wanted

Abigail is a mother of two, a wife, a daughter, and a home-based entrepreneur who left her job because she wanted to spend more time with her children and aging mom. She lost her dad two years earlier, and she treasures her time with her mom.

Everyone thinks Abigail has the perfect life now that she works for herself. *What could be better than spending each day doing what you love while being able to be there for the children?* What others do not know is that Abigail constantly struggles; she learns that working for one's self isn't always the best for one's personal and professional life. She realizes that as an entrepreneur, she has to be even more disciplined than when she was in the corporate world. She needs to be sure that when, where, and how she is spending her time and energy are serving her well. After all—when you are "the boss"—the good, bad, and ugly of the business ends with you.

Abigail realizes more than anyone else that if you are the business owner, you have to care for it almost as if it was a living organism. She still struggles with telling her family members that she can't do things with them when she is rushing for a deadline—or has overcommitted in order to tide herself over the lull seasons.

An entrepreneur, more than anyone else, is at risk of burnout. But any 24-Hour Woman can become consumed entirely with work if she is not consciously designing and living by the choices she makes.

Meet...

Let me ask you: does this schedule look familiar?

6:00 a.m.—The beeping alarm clock startles her into reality. It's time to get up, but she presses snooze. *Just five more minutes*, she thinks to herself.

6:05 a.m.—The alarm beeps again. *I will just skip the gym for today*, she thinks. *I have plenty of time before I need to get up.*

6:10 a.m.—BEEP-beep-beep. The thoughts running through her head now are: *I'm so tired...so sleepy...I had a late night call, so it's okay...I can sleep.* There goes the snooze button again.

6:15 a.m.—BEEP-BEEP-beep. *I need to get up, skip the gym today, hit the shower, and put on my contacts. Then, I'll change into my power suit...yes, the red one for today...and then I'll get breakfast ready.* She runs through her to-do list before she goes back to slumber-land once again.

6:20 a.m.—BEEP-BEEP-BEEP. It's serious now. She gets out of bed and hopes that the kids are still asleep. She could do a lot with a few more minutes to herself. *"Where is my ME time?"* she wonders aloud.

6:30 a.m.—Hitting the shower, getting dressed, and applying makeup in record time, she lets the dog out and gets busy in the kitchen.

7:00 a.m.—Child A wakes up. *Oh no, the breakfast is not ready... neither is the lunch box; and oh, the bus will arrive in thirty minutes,* she thinks to herself. "Just wash up and put your school clothes on by yourself," she shouts out to her child from the kitchen.

7:10 a.m.—Child A has his breakfast in front of the television, while Child B gobbles down his breakfast as he focuses on his handheld game. *Thank goodness they are quiet,* she thinks, as it dawns on her that she has not had a good conversation with her children for a long time. *But*, she thinks, *this is not the time. We need to hurry.*

7:30 a.m.—Hurrah...the bus is here. She propels the kids out the door with a quick kiss.

7:45 a.m.—She checks to ensure that she has everything she needs for work.

7:55 a.m.—While commuting to work, she realizes…the meat is not out of the freezer for the evening dinner, the sink is not cleared of dirty dishes, and she has not read the report for her morning meeting.

What a start to the day. But it's not too bad, she thinks. *At least the school bus was on time, the red suit was picked up from the cleaner's two days ago, and none of the children were sick.*

Yes, the to-do list is getting checked off; yes, she is staying busy; and yet, as the day unfolds, she does not feel like she is interacting with it in a meaningful manner. She is not progressing in the projects that mean the most to her, and yet all too soon, the end of the day arrives.

Do any of the above situations—or a combination of them—sound like *your life*? Are you, like some of the women in these highlighted stories, constantly trying to juggle your demands from both work and life? This is the state of daily living for many—just trying to cope with life's challenges and to-dos.

How, then, can one with just twenty-four hours *manage it all, navigate the issues of work and life—AND find happiness?*

The 24-Hour Woman Defined

In the Introduction, we explored the idea that *each of us has twenty-four hours in a single day; why is it that some women find success, happiness, and fulfillment in their days—while others discover only frustration and fatigue?* Let's recap:

We live in a highly mobile and always on, 24/7 society. Our modern, hectic, and sometimes chaotic environment forces us to commit to more, thus forcing us to squeeze more out of each day. Whether you are a working mom coping with kids and a career, a caregiver juggling between the needs of a dependent and your work, a thriving and multi-talented entrepreneur taking

*on the world, or a baby boomer without the possibility of true "retirement,"
this book is for you—offering a tool to build the beautiful tapestry of your
legacy amidst of the challenge of your hectic and sometimes chaotic life.*

*Why now? With career opportunities abounding in business, and our
culture and society transforming in the last decade, now is the opportune
time to pull back the curtains to unveil a vibrant and joyous life. Technology
(new social media and collaborative systems that allow telecommuting
and flexible work), demographic shifts (gender and generation shifts that
increase the number of women in the workplace as the population ages), and
globalization (the world feeling a lot smaller than it once did) have changed
the context of business and the workplace. These shifts provide new options
for women to plug in, literally, to new careers and work setups—locally,
regionally, and internationally.*

*The book serves to reinforce her, as stated in the Introduction: The
24-Hour Woman is one who recognizes her challenges and is equipped to
enjoy her work-life-play optimally, taking into consideration the well-being
of herself as well as those with whom she is in relationship. This could include
children, a spouse, extended family, coworkers, a boss, clients, and more.
The 24-Hour Woman is no longer daunted by the challenges around her,
but instead inspired by them—because she is equipping herself with time-
tested and cutting-edge strategies and tools, embracing the right attitudes,
and creating her own success of joy and vibrancy as she journeys towards her
life destiny.*

Three Myths of the 24-Hour Woman

Before we proceed, let's explore the three main myths associated with
today's 24-Hour Woman. These myths may keep women trapped in
their circumstances; but understanding and unraveling these myths can
free each woman to experience greater joy and vibrancy.

**Myth #1: The 24-Hour Woman Has All of the Resources at
Her Disposal.** The truth of the matter is, the 24-Hour Woman is

"STRESSED" like the rest of women, having a thousand tasks on her to-do list; but she is mindful that she can't do it all alone. Whether at work, at home, or engaging in her personal life, she actively cultivates additional support before she desperately needs it. This means creating support systems at work and in her community or family.

Myth #2: The 24-Hour Woman Can Have It All. The 24-Hour Woman has the wisdom to know that *managing it all* does not mean *having it all*. Rather, it means achieving satisfaction and happiness in areas that matter most. Instead of trying to do and have everything, the 24-Hour Woman masters the art of navigating life successfully by focusing first on the legacy she wants to build.

Myth #3: The 24-Hour Woman is Successful When She Emulates What She Sees in the Advertisements and Media. The 24-Hour Woman is high achieving on her own terms and not as defined by society or the media. She knows what's important to her and sets her heart on it.

We will bust these and more myths in Chapter 3 as we dissect them and empower you with new rules of the game. First, we are going to

☀   ☀   ☀

"I think they're (urban women professionals) increasingly more influential in their society and their professions, and also they play a very important role in their families, the carryover of their values, also the transformations of those values. But also at the same time, they're under a lot of pressure from work and from family burdens, from children rearing."
—**Yang Lan**, CEO, Sun Media,
referring to urban women professionals in China
(CNN.com, *"Interview with Yang, Lan,"* October 24, 2007).

☀   ☀   ☀

address some of the anxiety and fear that comes from realizing that your position needs to change.

Five Steps to Re-Packing Your Skills for a New Role

As you begin to lift the veil on your current job and position yourself as a 24-Hour Woman, you may realize that your current job is not the one you will have for long. You may, in fact, realize that your job is about to be phased out of existence.

One question I'm often asked is what to do if "the job that I have now is no longer going to exist in twelve months." If you are about to transition—or be transitioned—out of your job, you need to take a different lens to defining your role. Begin to see your role as *no longer just your title*, but as *a combination of the deliverables you provide.* Your first step in navigating this change—whether desired or unexpected—is to unbundle all of the wonderful knowledge, skills, and experiences you have so that you can uncover options and opportunities.

I never fail to feel amazement when I hear the squeal of delight at our "StepUp for Women Program" as a participant jumps with joy knowing that she is not stuck or even at a dead end; in fact, this may very well be her new beginning! How many times have you heard a similar story of an entrepreneur who started a successful business only after losing a job? **There is opportunity in the ashes, but your success depends upon your ability to reframe your career value based on your long-term strategy.**

Rather than reacting to short-term change, the 24-Hour Woman creates long-term change by living mindfully through transitions. Follow these steps:

1. **Make a list of ALL of your knowledge, skills, and experience for ALL paid and non-paid roles.**

2. **Make a list of ALL of the latest training or learning that you have gathered.**

3. **Make a list of your top five areas of interest.** Don't judge or censor yourself; just write them down. If you are unsure, ask yourself: *What do I love to do in my free time? What magazines do I love to read?*

4. **Put your knowledge, skills, and experience into broad categories** (see Putting It Into Practice sidebar).

5. **Make a list of all possibilities and options of roles in your area of interest.**

Putting It Into Practice

Let's explore *knowledge, skills, and experience* by using a human resource professional as an example. After all, I did spend nearly a decade in this field before I became an entrepreneur! So what can we unravel from the perspective of knowledge, skills, and experience of someone serving in HR? Note the transferable skills in these six broad categories:

- **Communication Skills: Expressing, Transmitting, and Interpreting Knowledge.** Specific communication skills pertaining to HR may include delivering presentations, public speaking, writing, listening, giving feedback, editing, and facilitating discussions.

- **Research & Planning: Searching for Information and Understanding and Preparing for Future Needs.** Skills in this area related to HR include resource identification, analysis, creative visualization, goal setting, problem solving, and defining needs. These are essential skills to conceptualize business issues into models and present solutions that offer holistic approaches.

- **Human Resources: Support, Motivation, Counseling Others, Delegation, and Offering Empathy.**
- **Organization, Management, and Leadership: Supervision, Direction, and Guidance of Others to Achieve Goals.** Specific skills related to HR include coordinating tasks, teaching, coaching, selling ideas or products, managing groups, and resolving conflict.
- **Work Survival: Basic Survival Skills Needed Anywhere.** Related to HR skills, this includes effective time management, attention to detail, organization, and decision-making.
- **Diversity and Inclusion: Ability to Work with Clients and Team Members Across Different Cultures, Genders, Generations, and Industries.** Specific to HR, this includes possessing adaptability. Especially for those who travel often, adapting well lends itself to the skill of networking or being in new situations or environments.

There you have it: a list of possible roles that you can explore!

Taking It Home: Five Steps to Ensuring Meals Are Prepared with Tender, Loving Care

As a working mom, while you are concerned about your career, you undoubtedly also are concerned about your family at home. One of the key challenges I initially had was to ensure that for at least one meal per day, at the end of the day, my family would come together and have a nutritious, home-cooked meal. This is not an expectation of everyone, nor is this for everyone—particularly in Singapore where good meals are available almost twenty-four hours a day in food centers. I love to cook, however, so one of the ways I can show my family how much I love them is to prepare their meals.

One question I have been asked frequently is *how can we prepare at least one meal a day for our families?* Here are my five steps to making these meals a reality. (You may also download the checklist and planning chart for this at www.The24HourWoman.com/Resources)

1. **Engage in the one-time effort of researching all of the wonderful dishes that your family (and you) love.**

2. **Categorize the recipes according to the meal type (such as beef dishes, fish dishes, vegetables, and so on).** Categorize them further according to cooking time and methods (steamed, fried, baked, deep fried, stir fried, etc.).

3. **Develop your meal plans for the next seven days based on your work demands.** Some meals may be more elaborate than others, depending upon the amount of time required and level of help you have in the kitchen (such as from your children and/or spouse).

4. **Go grocery shopping once a week, armed with the general idea of which dishes you plan to prepare.**

5. **Give your family members some choices and control in the process.** For example, you may have decided that Monday night's entrée will be chicken. You can't easily rush out to shop at the last minute to change the entrée based upon new whims. You can, however, allow your family members a choice of having the chicken prepared by steaming, baking, frying, etc.— you get the idea. Provide options for them based upon the fine balance between preparation time and what might appeal to your family.

Prepared with tender loving care, I am sure your family would love having a home-cooked meal prepared for them each day—or with whatever frequency you can achieve. Try this planning method, and see if it would save you time and effort for an altogether satisfying meal with your family.

What other tips or ideas do you have regarding cooking meals at home? Email me at solutions@The24HourWoman.com. I would love to hear your ideas, and I am sure you will inspire and encourage others.

The 24-Hour Woman Speaks

Ms. Patsy Doerr (US)

Global Head, Diversity & Inclusion/Corporate Responsibility

Thomson Reuters

Being one of the first women to enter a two-hundred-fifty-year-old all men's college was just the start of Patsy Doerr's mark on a male-centric workplace. Throughout her career, Patsy has exemplified her natural ability to lead others. She was placed in environments where the odds were stacked against her. Patsy used the five Foundational Pillars of a 24-Hour Woman in two different circumstances in her life. (You will discover these in more depth for yourself in Chapter 5. Be patient; you are uncovering much in these interviews that you will later apply to your own development!) Patsy recently described in an interview with me for my "Conversations with Uncommon Women" series her role in two male-dominated environments, both of which inspired her to use her skills to her advantage to create a *life most excellent* for herself.

At the age of eighteen, Patsy attended the Washington and Lee University, which at the time was an all-men's college. She was among one hundred women who attended the school with fifteen hundred men. It's easy to see the difficulties she could have faced in this very male-dominated environment. Instead, Patsy appreciated her situation and realized that there were many opportunities available to her—which could also open more doors for the few other women who attended that college. She accepted that she might face many unique challenges in the process of achieving her goals, but she also had the awareness to know that she could make a difference—not only in her own college experience, but also for all women in the university.

Patsy's awareness allowed her to seek opportunities to enhance women's influence on her community. Patsy shared:

> *I think there are two ways in which the female voice was heard. Number one, we spent a lot of time connecting with the men and with the alumni, and actually it was a very interesting exercise that led me down the path I took: going into a primarily all-men's industry and financial services as well. It is really understanding the style and thinking of the men at the university and, as I said, the alumni as well. I think the second way we were heard is that we really went in and built a number of new initiatives. Again, one, I am an athlete. I enjoy sports quite a bit, so we started a basketball team. We started a speech team. We started sororities, actually from the ground up. Basically, we had enough opportunity to build things— again, from the ground up—that actually added value to the university. The university is heavily focused on engagement and alumni connections, and so all of these programs actually helped build that community.*

Patsy used her environment to leverage her skills and applied them in constructive ways to get her voice heard. She applied those same skills later in life—during her career. As she stated in our interview, having that experience in college pushed her towards a male-dominated career.

As she left college, she already possessed the skills to put her mark on an environment that brought many obstacles for women. After college, Patsy entered the business field, which was completely new to her. Her career path had changed since college, and she decided to go into business, even though she had no education or experience in it. This could have thrown a lot of obstacles at her, but instead of looking at ways she could fail, Patsy appreciated her situation. She knew that no matter how little experience or skills she had in her chosen field, she still wasn't starting at ground zero. She knew that she possessed skills in working with men in a male-dominated field, and she used them to her advantage.

Patsy started her career in sales, and then transitioned to investment banking at JP Morgan. It, again, was a completely new field, but she took the opportunity and was thrown into the derivatives trading desk. There, she was asked to develop learning and development programs for the traders. She knew nothing about the product, but she basically built a learning curriculum for their derivative university.

Although Patsy knew there were risks involved with this career path, she had the awareness to know that she could do it. She was aware that even if challenges presented themselves, she had skills to fall back on. That acceptance eventually led her to action. Patsy earned her master's degree at night at Fordham University in organizational development. She was able to apply what she had learned at night to her work the next day. She knew that she could advance in her field, even though the odds were against her. She actively sought experiences that would develop her skills—and eventually lead to higher positions in her field.

Patsy went on to work for Deutsche Bank in the UK. There, she started a learning and development function for operations in an IT part of the organization. She also was asked to develop a graduate training program across the entire Deutsche Bank organization.

When she came back to the United States, she worked for Credit Suisse. The organization lacked learning and development, so she built an infrastructure and framework around people development. Patsy then transitioned to running and building a leadership development curriculum for her managing directors, which was called the Leadership Institute. Patsy's most drastic change came after a conversation with her boss. He asked her if she would move to Asia to build the talent function for Credit Suisse. She eagerly accepted the opportunity and moved her husband and two children to Hong Kong.

If you look at Patsy's career path, you can witness an obvious pattern of working in fields in which she initially had no experience. When asked about this decision, Patsy said:

> *Generally my orientation is to drive on new experiences. If we were to reflect on adult learning, my learning style was very much about learning from experience. I also enjoyed taking risks, albeit, mitigated risks, all within the context of large corporations that were very stable from the beginning but also had that newness factor to them. For me, jumping into a new experience is how I learn, how I thrive, where I get my energy from, and actually what inspires me on a daily basis.*

In both of these circumstances, Patsy used the five Foundational Pillars (which we will elaborate on in Chapter 5) to create a life that sparked her passion. When asked to define success, Patsy explained that her original definition of success was very much focused on upward movements. She was excited to thrive in her career, and she kept striving for the next bigger role. That is still important to her today, but she also defines success as *doing work that inspires her*. She feels successful when she is passionate about her work—and finds rewards in the responsibilities that come with it.

Would you like to watch the full interview with Patsy? Come on over to www.The24HourWoman.com/blog. Share your comments and ask your questions; I would love to hear from you.

Launching Ahead: Are You Ready to Become a 24-Hour Woman?

In this chapter, we've learned a bit about what it means to be a 24-Hour Woman. *Who needs to learn the secrets of the 24-Hour Woman?*

- **Anyone who loves living life to the fullest.**
- **Those who know there is more to life than the to-do list.**
- **Those who hunger to find and live their destinies— one day looking back with pride at the legacies they have built.**
- **I suspect that includes you!**

There are ways to live above all of these daily challenges without forgetting our destinies. There are ways to *manage it all and find happiness and fulfillment.* Re-arranging priorities and effective time management will provide only partial relief. A new approach is needed: the approach of the 24-Hour Woman, which is based on research—and results from my students' and my own life. Those who know the tools of the 24-Hour Woman will thrive in their lives; those who don't will continue to struggle. **Do you want to:**

- **Spend quality time with your family?**
- **Learn and grow?**
- **Have fun? Achieve success, happiness, and more?**

Join thousands of others, and me, on "The 24-Hour Woman Revolution" towards a vibrant, joyful life that fulfills your destiny. The time is now; **read on!**

In Chapter 2 and beyond, we will share more actions that others have taken to gain big advantages in living vibrant and joyous lives as 24-Hour Women. *You can be one of these women, too!*

Signpost for Chapter 1

Get your journals, and get ready for your journey of growth. Now, consider these questions as you reflect on Chapter 1:

1. What does success mean to you?
2. What myths have you adopted that are holding you back from thriving as a 24-Hour Woman?
3. How much massive action have you taken toward living a vibrant and joyful life?

Chapter 2

MY STORY

"The power plant has no energy. It generates energy."
—**Brendon Burchard**

*U*pon graduation, I was an economics and statistics major, but that is not where my heart was. It was just something I did because of my studies. My first role in the corporate arena was in a manufacturing firm. The situation there was unique because, in those days, it was rare to find a female leading a Japanese firm. (May I add, it's still rare to see female executives taking the lead in Japanese firms. But my experience working in a typically male-dominated industry gave me hope that there was a role for women—including women in corporate leadership.) That's where I got started. I learned a lot about managing across cultures—about managing relationships and people. As a rookie right out of school, there was so much to learn.

My passion for learning is something that I brought along with me throughout my career, and still use to this day. The desire to learn—and the passion to be curious—added to my competence, experience, and exposure (even if it meant sitting through tough and painful technology-platform-related tutorials). But most of all, all of these learning experiences added to my own repertoire of perspectives.

My Rollercoaster Ride

I learned so much in the manufacturing environment. As fresh graduates, we thought that surely promotions and bonuses would come our way. But that would not become the reality if we did not manage our careers wisely. I went out and looked for help; and in that day and age, help came in the form of books. There was no Internet available. I loved to read (and still do!), so I read a lot about women in careers and women entrepreneurs. I read a lot about career management and leadership.

Unfortunately, many of the books available were written by men for men, so I started to study women entrepreneurs in terms of their leadership. I studied the examples set by the leaders of companies like Mary Kay and Estée Lauder. I knew that I didn't want to be a Margaret Thatcher kind of leader; I didn't want to lead *like a man*, because I didn't think that would have been authentic to me or sustainable. Instead, I wanted to lead collaboratively. I looked to role models to see how I might emulate them, while being authentic to my own style. I started to ask questions to derive the keys to their success: How did they start a business? How did they sustain their beliefs in themselves and abilities to support themselves in business? My resulting discoveries really started a foundation of skills that I eventually applied in creating our current "StepUp for Women" program—a women's leadership and career management program.

Twenty-four months down the road, I was ready to move on to a totally different industry. And I did—to an industry called *retail*. Retail was and is so dynamic. It's fast moving, and everything is happening on the go—which is a bit different from manufacturing in terms of its business cycle. In my role in advertising and promotions, I looked into marketing products across different generations. When I look back, that's where my interest in generational dynamics started. I was curious: Why did the youth like certain things whereas so-called adults did not? The consumer behavior of different generations was interesting to me, and so I studied it.

Being in retail opened my eyes to a totally different world. It exposed me to such experiences as what it takes to put together a fashion show in a big arena like a ballroom or expo. It got me involved in working with designers so that I could be inspired by their creativity, which is something that I bring with me even today as I work with my distributed team. In fact, I developed a love for learning and working across disciplines with different people. The ability to appreciate such diversity is something that I also retain today—helping me in my career journey and business.

Retail has its perils, too—such as long work hours. I began to plan for a different role. Eventually, I left retail to join a company called International SOS, which is a medical evacuation company that sets up and runs call centers and medical centers around the globe. Once again, I was immersed into a totally different field from what I had done previously.

International SOS is a French firm. So I went from a local Japanese firm to a French firm, which was a change in culture. This movement gave me the chance for an even wider range of exposure—working in different global cultures and working with different people—including women (who would become the eventual audience for whom I would become passionate to work). I was fortunate to learn from my experiences with professionally trained women and women leaders. I examined and admired how they approached business, how they approached work, how they approached their function, and how they managed their family lives—in places such as Japan, Korea, China, and Kazakhstan. **My observations over time gave me the insight to say, "Hey, although there are challenges that we think are different, wc also face many similarities."**

That experience added to my collective perspectives of women in business/work, women in leadership, and women in dual roles (being work and family/personal life focused). I, myself, came to a point where I had a dual role dilemma. I was running a global function, and my fiancé—and now husband—was also in a global role. We had to take out our calendars and schedule our dates based on geography, or they wouldn't happen. For example, we asked one another, "Which continent are you going to be on during the upcoming Valentine's Day?" We literally had to sit down and mark our schedules to find a time when we could share a day together. When we decided to get married, I felt that one of us should stay put in Singapore. I decided that I would be the one to make that change.

I had really loved all of my roles since graduation up until that point. I had learned so much in each of them. I had grown so much, and I had met many people who I was blessed to have support me—a factor I'll talk more about later. **I realized through this experience that at times, the choice becomes not just about work, but about work-life.**

I chose to take on a local role, and I joined a women's and children's hospital. Again, very uniquely, I was guided there. I stayed close to nine years because there was a lot of opportunity for growth and movement. My bosses were very open, and they were very empowering. They saw something in me that I didn't realize in myself. They saw a bigger potential that I didn't see. *They believed in me.*

In the hospital, I was hired for an HR role for which I had no formal training. Previously, I had been running operations or corporate communications or advertising. I don't know why, but they chose me for this healthcare HR role. Healthcare is a very challenging environment. In addition, I'm not medically trained; I'm not a medical doctor, practitioner, pharmacist, nor nurse practitioner. As an administrator in healthcare, I would have to demonstrate my credibility. What could I bring to the table in a healthcare setting? *You can't start up a team or do an operation if you have no doctors or nurses or surgeons. But you can certainly do so without an administrator.* That's what I thought was probably running through their minds when they looked at me.

Is the Grass Greener on the Other Side?

In my time at the hospital, I had to learn how to build credibility, how to build my sphere of influence, and how to manage their business—*our* business. I also learned what their concerns were and how to be seen as part of their team to add value to their intent. **Being in this workplace, I found that success is largely about what you bring to the table as a team to influence the final outcome—the *common* outcome desired by that team.** That concept of teamwork had always been a major philosophy in my life—and still is.

The reason that I set up my business, LifeWorkz, was because I wanted a greater sphere of influence in the corporate arena, so as to empower company leaders to believe that they could create more contemporary and engaging workplaces. The healthcare setting where I worked for nine years was an absolutely wonderful place, because my supervisor then—Jennifer Lee, MD, the CEO of the healthcare institution for the women and children's hospital (who is now one of my mentors)—was and is a true women of influence. **She has always believed that we all want to be great in our jobs and that her role is to remove the obstacles that stand in the way of our success. Doing** so, she believes, ultimately will lead to an organization's success. Yes, she is very "Edward Deming" in philosophy—in that she believes people will do their best when they are empowered.

We all want to deliver a good piece of work. The question is: what are we doing as leaders to remove the barriers from people so that they can succeed in their tasks? When I started my business, that was my objective—to help companies build more inspiring and empowering workplaces. I started, of course, from the examination of what work-life issues existed within those companies, because when I spent time in that healthcare setting, I experienced firsthand how we were able to leverage our work-life strategies to attract, retain, and engage our healthcare providers. Given that these workers were in short supply globally, our leadership knew that effectively managing our talent was crucial to our organization's success.

We were able to retain those workers and motivate them. To top off that success, we experienced great customer feedback. Additionally, engagement of non-medical staff went up because they felt that they could cope more effectively with their work and non-work responsibilities.

Bear in mind that, in this healthcare setting, we crossed different cultures. In terms of gender, 85 percent of my workforce was women. I also had to manage the engagement of five different generations within the hospital. What work-life strategies helped us attract, retain, motivate and engage them? I realized that work-life strategies could be effective in a corporate setting, but their success required that individuals make the decisions to prioritize and implement them.

I asked myself: *what work-life strategies would empower them to strive in life?* This experience got me back to my first love—or my first calling—of working with women. This is also when I decided that I eventually wanted to start my own business. I knew the timing wasn't right for me to venture out on my own, but I saw that the future would reflect cultural, gender, and generational diversity. I also saw that the role of men and women would evolve—both at work and at home. I wanted to be a bigger part of that movement.

It was not like I jumped out of bed one day and said, "I'm going to start my own business." Instead, the desire was triggered at one of my performance reviews with my supervisor (and now mentor) Dr. Lee. It grew from there—starting as a small seed. She asked me, "Cheryl, are you going to spend the rest of your career in health care?" That got me thinking, because I was very, very close to the ten-year mark in my journey in the healthcare setting, and I'd never stayed that long in an organization. I asked myself: *why should I stay?* Some of my peers who I saw across the globe had to make tough choices. Some left the workforce altogether or had to change to different jobs that they didn't really love or which were in conflict with who they wanted to be. Some of those choices forced them to make decisions between family and work. I realized I had stayed because it was about the workplace, the culture, and the leadership of the company I worked for; those factors had made all the difference.

My transition also was not about just waking up and having a great idea. But at the same time, I was prompted rather strongly one morning while doing my Bible study. I was reading about how God called Abraham to leave where he was, and Abraham left. Abraham did not question and ask, "God, where am I going?" He trusted, and he took action. The business idea was brewing within me, and this study stirred it in my consciousness. *If Abraham could do it, why wouldn't I?* That idea sat with me for a very long time.

This whole idea of setting up my own business took me three years to implement—from that time of prompting by my boss/supervisor, Dr. Lee, to the prompting that I had in the Bible passage about Abraham. The outcome of these experiences was compounded by the motivation I received from different people who came to me and said, "You should help my company become more effective or come and see how my workplace can become more engaging."

To fast forward to today, never in my entire life did I imagine that I would be in a business that required me to be an expert in my field—to speak, consult, train, and research. Now that I am doing it, and have done it for several years, I can attest that it is challenging to work across different cultures, because in a lot of people's perspective, being a petite Chinese woman is not an advantage amongst the global field of "experts." Yes, I speak English, yet English is not my first language. I grew up speaking several languages, so in a sense, there are many odds stacked against me. I never thought that I would be running the business I am right now (or publishing my book). But it was a prompting that took hold deep within me, and it distilled for about three years. The promptings of my calling, combined with the previous jobs or roads I had taken, were not coincidental. My experience was unique, and there were certain things I needed to learn in the process—through my exposure to different cultures, working across different generations, and working with women groups. This all accumulated to create LifeWorkz, and in more recent years, my work with women professionals and entrepreneurs.

After running LifeWorkz and helping organizations, I chose to start a second business of working with women, because the more I worked in inspiring workplaces, **the more I saw that no matter how companies had their policies and cultures in place, individuals still needed to make many conscious choices to design their own lives.** I chose to work with women because I've walked their path. I have three boys, and I've acquired my master's degree. I've done my studies. I've worked in a corporate setting on a full-time basis. I've started my own business.

I would never have been able to do all of that if I did not have support at home from my husband, my family, my sister, and my parents. I also had support in the workplace, and not just by learning the cultural aspect, but also from my supervisor and boss, my teammates—and now in my business, from my clients. I don't take any of that for granted. I came to the point where I admitted that I wanted to work with women because I had walked the path of the corporate world successfully, I had a corporate crossover, and I was (and still am) enjoying my role as an entrepreneur. I wanted to share my experiences with other women who may be encountering similar challenges and opportunities.

If we think that by starting our own businesses, we will have more freedom—well, think again. We will still need to consciously set boundaries and make choices. That's where I feel I can offer my greatest input to women globally; my vision is to help them live more vibrant and joyful lives through making conscious decisions about what they want out of life. I thrive on helping them make the big pieces fall into place and build the habits that will support them on a day-to-day basis.

I would say that my entire journey in the corporate arena, and then crossing over and into entrepreneurship, came about through appreciating the people, workplaces, roles, and skills I have encountered or developed. Being aware of them and what they mean has allowed me to ask what it would take for me to start my own business.

But beyond the support I've received, **the greatest piece of the puzzle that started my success as a 24-Hour Woman, I think, is my faith or belief in the legacy I want to leave behind.** That's where I always start, and it drives me forward. What is the legacy you want to leave behind?

"We need to understand that there is no formula for how women should lead their lives. That is why we must respect the choices that each woman makes for herself and her family. Every woman deserves the chance to realize her God-given potential."
—**Hillary Rodham Clinton**, It Takes a Village

What Do I Want My Legacy to Be?

You may be destined for great things, but if you do not consciously move in their direction, you might just miss building that legacy that you want to leave behind. It took me three years to take that first step to be able to say, "Yes, I want to be an entrepreneur, and I want to work with companies," and then eventually, "I want to work specifically with women groups—and with women globally." The process has been challenging, but I totally love what I do, and I want to be able to empower and work with other women to give them the same ability to evolve and create their own *lives most excellent*—wherein they thrive in work/business and life.

It feels like a very long time since I started Lifeworkz, and yet I find myself continually reinventing it. As I searched out a different business model, LifeWorkz's business shifted to leverage on technology. This provided us with the ability to extend our reach globally to companies and all of their subsidiaries. It also gave me the ability to revisit my first love of working with women to empower them, regardless of their environment and circumstances. And that is where I am today.

The question I seek to help women answer today is: *in spite of the twenty-four hours we have, and in spite of us having different challenges at different life stages and career stages, how can we still thrive in business/work and life?* And I see the momentum building around this question, because there is more consciousness now; we know that there should be more to life than just work. We also are aware of who is paying the price if we are consumed economically only by our work. My legacy is to influence—to garner momentum with women from all walks of life to consciously design their lives towards their legacies.

My family has been very supportive of my career transitions. I would say that the first people who I am very thankful for and appreciative of are my parents. From the very beginning, when I graduated from school, they supported me going into a so-called non-traditional workplace. They had always wanted me to become a teacher, because they believed that the public sector would provide a very stable job. When I chose to go into the corporate arena, my parents and teachers were a bit apprehensive, but still very supportive—and they have been since, in every single endeavor (even in my madness of doing a corporate crossover to become an entrepreneur!). They worry, I know, but they are supportive in helping me however they can. They were instrumental in keeping an eye on my kids when they were much younger, and my husband and I had to travel due to work. Although now, we do less of that, because instead of looking at Valentine's Day locations, my husband and I will look at our schedules and try to ensure that at least one of us is home with the children while the other travels.

My husband has been wonderful. He knows that this is what I'm passionate about, and he helps me in my business by helping me in finance and technology, in working with the boys, and in really supporting me in the different ways I need to be successful. In addition to my husband and parents, my sister has also been very supportive. My boys, too, have been wonderful. They miss me when I travel, but we leverage technology—Skype or FaceTime on our iPhones when possible or Google Hangout. They have also, from young ages, learned to be responsible and independent. They are guided by, very thankfully, the values that have been inculcated in them when they were young, and they are bearing fruit in their lives right now. That's one of my greatest thanksgivings. Overall, in these ways, I would say that I have been very blessed, because the support that I needed up front, and on an ongoing basis with my family, has always been there for me.

I took a lot of risks when I made those choices for my life and for the legacy I wanted to leave. I don't think risk taking is something that, perhaps in the Asian culture, we traditionally emphasize much. I think the world has changed, however, and our context also has changed. Things that were deemed to be certain do not seem to be as certain anymore. I'm not asking you to be reckless, but I think it's important to take risks, particularly if you have strong convictions to do so. Every strategic decision that you take involves risk. Only decisions that are made on autopilot do not.

Our modeling doesn't stop with ourselves. With the values that we have as adults, we have the opportunity to teach the youth and children under our watch. We can help them, too, make the right decisions about who they are and what their destinies are. That's another reason why I am very enthused about working with women, because when we equip women well, we know that they will influence their families, societies, and communities. I am passionate about working hand in hand with them to impact their societies in positive and optimistic ways—to bring a sense of hope and development and counter the number of social issues that many of us see right now in our communities.

Women have a strong role in influencing children. Not just as moms, but also as individuals who are in contact with children and youth. The next generation will gain influence from the people around them, so that they can go back and influence their families.

Five Steps to Re-Launching Your Career

You may be one who left the workplace to care for the young or an elderly adult, and now are looking at re-launching back into the workplace. Many women pause their careers for caregiving responsibilities—whether for childcare, elder care, or to pursue some other interests outside a traditional career trajectory. So many stories like this have come to my attention.

Here are five proven steps that have enabled many to return to part-time or full-time work:

1. **Build your confidence.** Build habits and get into activities that get you back on your feet to your position of strength. Increase your dose of adventure. Take on a brand new adventure of learning new things or taking on new roles (for example, try swimming if you don't swim, or give 100 percent to learning a new hobby in your area of interest). Like the saying goes, *feel the fear, but do it anyway.* Fear is like a muscle that, when exercised and stretched beyond, builds confidence.

2. **Repackage your knowledge, skills, experience—paid or unpaid—even if just through volunteer work.** Determine whether you desire to transition back into your career track and if it will offer you the lifestyle you desire for this stage in life— or if you desire to work in a new career.

3. **Network and broaden your search for opportunities and fit.** Let people know your value and objectives through your elevator speech. I love using: "I help_____to do_____ so that_____." It illustrates your value and what you bring to an organization and team.

4. **Prepare and market yourself, and seize opportunities to work in your areas of strength.** Don't be afraid to start small and build from there. A friend of mine spent fourteen years looking after her two boys, leaving a very successful advertising and marketing career behind. While looking after the household needs, she also volunteered at her boys' school and at church—in addition to running a small home business in areas having to do with food, beverage, or events. As the boys grew older into their teenage years, she began to explore ways to get back "on the ramp." Instead of heading straight back to advertising and marketing, she examined what she wanted in her current life stage. She also considered the legacy she wanted to leave behind. Her great love for food and her big heart in demonstrating her love to others through her cooking led her to a role in teaching others to cook some of her favorite dishes in a culinary academy. Her legacy had to do with showing her passion and love through food. She did not want another "full-time" job in a traditional sense, so this was perfect, as she would work only twice a week, leaving time for her family. But she admitted that she needed to work up her courage so that she could teach and not just cook for others!

5. **Be open to new ways of work.** Many women were able to market themselves as "a company of one" based on their core competencies—and eventually were engaged as a full contributing member of a distributed team. The freelance world is set to explode as companies seek out the best talent and leverage on flexibility to engage with those individuals. Are you ready for this new world of work?

Remember, in everything you do, keep your family and loved ones close, and listen to their concerns. The transition may be hard for them too, and you will be better served if you ask for their participation early—by holding a meeting to discuss your plans, and following through by addressing any concerns they express. Ensure that proper support systems are in place throughout the process to navigate this transition.

I also encourage you to check out www.iRelaunch.com, which is a great resource for individuals seeking to return to the workplace.

Putting It Into Practice

Let's explore how we can re-launch our journeys back to the workplace. Here's Alice's story. She was one of our program participants, and is now also a friend. She spent ten years as a very successful financial analyst before leaving her position to care for her elderly father in the last three years of his life. While caring for her dad, she needed to learn about being a caregiver to an aging parent who was not well. In addition to attending workshops to learn what knowledge and skills she needed, she also volunteered her time in a retirement village as a fundraiser. While she was officially out of the workplace, she kept in touch with her peers and networked by attending industry events and touching base with those in the industry. When she was thinking of getting back into the workplace, she re-examined what she really wanted and came to the realization that THIS was her second chance to do what she really wanted. Let's examine how Alice tackled the five steps to re-launching her career:

- **Build your confidence.** Alice learned new skills on caregiving and what it took to run a facility like the retirement home.

- **Repackage your knowledge, skills, experience— paid or unpaid—even if just through volunteer work.** This was simple for Alice. She easily listed her management, analytical, and people skills that were transferrable.

- **Network and broaden your search for opportunities and fit.** Alice reflected through her journals and realized that she really loved the work and time spent in the retirement village. She loved seeing the smiles and joy in the eyes of the elders that she encountered. She also felt their pain and disappointment when their families did not care for them anymore. She decided that what she wanted to do next was re-launch her career—into a role that would contribute to the well-being of the elderly. So she started her search amongst hospitals, retirement villages, and elder care centers. She even considered starting her own home care service.

- **Prepare and market yourself, and seize opportunities to work in your areas of strength.** Alice started as a part-time administrator within a retirement village, although she had no former experience in this area except as a volunteer. Given her drive and focus on her vision, she eventually landed a senior operations manager role—having had the opportunity to prove herself as a part-timer.

Be open to explore brand new skills and roles you have never heard of, because those that you know or have had previous knowledge of may not be in existence any more.

Challenges as an Entrepreneur

Financing

Throughout my career, I thought in terms of challenges—what might be standing in my way? Or another way to frame this is that I asked myself: what's my "mind block"? There was a lot to learn about aspects of business I formerly had taken for granted, which was challenging because I'd always been a specialist.

Learning how to run a business was key (and now it is one of the key pieces that I focus on in my work with women who are transiting from the corporate arena to being entrepreneurs). One challenge I discovered in moving out of the corporate arena and into my own business was financial, because when coming from a corporate background into being a sole entrepreneur, I realized that the deep pockets weren't there anymore. Financing was a key piece for me on an ongoing basis. When I started to transition to leverage more on technology, it was a business model that not many people were open to at the time, and I therefore was not about to take a bank loan. Instead, I overcame the challenge by talking to friends and family who funded an extension of the business.

Small Is Beautiful?

The other challenge I faced was that my distributed team comprised a small and local/regional firm. What company would want to engage us? We found a solution in being agile and really getting to know our clients—building our credibility and reputation with them. We've since had the good fortune of working with many global firms. And guess what? Many of them *came to us*. I believe God opened the doors for us, and that was His way of providing for us. When we asked these companies later, "We (as a distributed team) are not a big global consulting firm; why did you come to us?" they'd tell us, "Because we liked that you were niched, you were small and agile, and you really 'got it.' You got to know us as your clients, and you did not give us a cookie-cutter solution."

So that's where Lifeworkz was unique, specifically in how we worked with our clients—and still do. We see what their issues are, and based on the latest research and circumstances, we design the solution—*with* them.

So, back to my challenge of financing, the solution was found in getting the word out and getting clients. That's how we, as entrepreneurs, can overcome.

Working ALL the Time

The third challenge comes from the fact that when you become an entrepreneur, you need to be very, very conscious about when it's work and when it's not work, because work/business can consume your life. As an entrepreneur, if you aren't careful, you'll always think about the business. My husband said to me one day, "You know, you are working more than when you were in the corporate arena." And that was not the intention, remember? The intention was to have better life effectiveness. You should realize by now that I totally enjoyed and was passionate about what I did—and I still am to this day. I have no difficulty staying in that "world" for the longest time. **But I've learned that as entrepreneurs, we need to be even more conscious about setting boundaries. My legacy is not just about my life's work, and I need my day-to-day actions to reflect that.**

I had to be very conscious about checking and consciously telling myself to hold myself accountable to boundaries—which included leaving time for the children, time with my husband, and time for a family vacation with my parents and sister. This accountability piece was a particular challenge for me, because number one, *I love what I do*, and number two, *I really want to give the best to the people I coach and companies I work with*. That takes time. To overcome this challenge, I've proactively looked at solutions to provide the same level of effectiveness with less time. This is one reason why going on a digital platform and utilizing social media was how I chose to grow the business.

Working more hours is a fairly common problem for entrepreneurs, and it still happens occasionally for me. That's why we have to be very conscious about it. We can't take our schedule for granted, particularly if our family is supportive of what we are doing. They will grant us some leeway; however, we must not think that working long hours is the new normal, or it will become our long-term reality and habit. As entrepreneurs, there are special circumstances, such as when launching a certain product or working with a certain client who is a bit more demanding. But we must always pull back and ask: *What's your legacy? What's your destination? Are you enjoying the journey?* Because if we don't, the work will consume us, and the overworked lifestyle will become acceptable—even when it is not. I think the process of setting boundaries around work-life is a work in progress. There are some clients I would love to have, but I know that it would just take too much out of me, and so I have to say no.

For example, putting together this book was not my forte. Writing is not my forte. But I knew it was a message I needed to find a way to get out to make it more accessible; if I had to spend an enormous amount of time and energy on it, I would. You need to weigh the costs and make sure that you are receiving a return on your investment that pays off—and preferably in terms of your long-term legacy.

Taking It Home: Three Ways to Building Strong Family Relations

As a working professional or entrepreneur, family support is important. This has been a cornerstone for me. This is an area that takes time to evolve and needs to be practiced consistently over time. In other words, it takes tremendous learning to find the right balance to keep family thriving in the midst of growing a business or career.

One question I have been asked frequently is: *how can we, in the midst of our busy lives and in a 24/7, social media crazy world, build strong family bonds?* **Here are my four ways to cultivating an environment for strong family bolds to flourish:** (You may also download the checklist and planning chart for this at www.The24HourWoman. com/Resources.)

1. **Speak well of and with respect for each family member.** I say this particularly in how one might speak about her husband in the presence of other members of the household. If there's anything I have learned in my marriage, it is to speak well and with respect about my husband. Only when there is unity between us will there be direction and foundation in the family. Having this rule in place also has helped me build a healthy relationship with my three boys. Practice public praise and private correction with family members regardless of age, because this builds good levels of self-esteem while allowing for growth due to private correction/disciplining.

2. **Train and teach family members their roles and their contribution to the family.** From the youngest to the oldest, help them see how they are valued members of the family. They should know that they can count on the family to be there, should they need any help or council. This creates a place of security from which they can take healthy risks in life to grow.

3. **Have fun.** Life is not all about being rigid in training. It's also about having fun as a family and building family-based experiences—whether they are traditions, family vacations, or jokes that are understood only by members of the household.

4. **Practice TLC—tender loving care—with your family relationships, and there will be love, joy, peace, and open communications amongst the members, because they know they are loved and respected for who they are.** (I know this can be challenging when raising a teenager or caring for a very opinionated elder.)

What other tips or ideas do you have to help build strong family relationships? Email me at solutions@The24HourWoman.com. I would love to hear your ideas, and I am sure you will inspire and encourage others.

 Signpost for Chapter 2

It's time to get your journals. Consider these questions as you reflect on Chapter 2:

1. Map out your career transitions. Identify what you liked or disliked in those roles.
2. What has your past career journey helped you discover about yourself—about who you are and who you desire to be?
3. How much massive action have you taken to become who you desire to be?

Chapter 3

MYTH BUSTING

"Right believing leads to right living."
—Joseph Prince

What Does *Having It All* Mean? Why Do You Want to *Have It All*?

$\mathscr{A}$ lot of talk has circulated about *having it all*. We've been challenged to do our best to achieve *it all*, but I would like to challenge us first to ask, "Why do we want to have it all?" *What does having it all bring to us?*

Some women who we have worked with seem so happy and fulfilled at the end of the day, and yet, from the naked eye, they don't seem to *have it all*, by society's standards. These women are not multi-millionaires. They may not have what we would deem as having it all—a great career with all of the trappings—but they live vibrant, joyful, and fulfilled lives. Or, they may be high achievers in their workplaces. **Yet despite being perfectly happy as high achievers and experts in competitive areas, they know that money comes second to fulfillment. Their passions and ideas of having it all stems from being** *excellent in what they do.* **They enjoy their relationships, and they have time for themselves and people who they care for.**

If we think we can have it all by comparing ourselves to others and what they may attribute to having it all, then we torture ourselves. But if we ask ourselves, "What does having it all mean, and what is it supposed to bring me?" then we define what having it all means. For example, one of my friends has a soon-to-be-released book that talks about her idea of having it all, which is really about minimizing distractions so that she can gain time and stay focused on her two young children. (See www.HandsFreeMama.com). Being there, being present, and being authentic with her children is more valuable to her than so-called *having it all.* Because while she might be running a busy schedule without clear boundaries in place, when she is with her children, she's not totally *with them.*

What does having it all mean to you, and do you have to have it all right now? That is one of the biggest challenges that you face, because if you want it right now, depending on your life stage, you will find so many interests competing for your valuable resources of time and energy—whether those interests are family, relationships, your business, or your health.

Does *Having It All* Mean *Having It All Right Now*?

I think that question is something that we need to work through as 24-Hour Women, and you will need to answer it for yourself. In every chapter of *The 24-Hour Woman,* we discuss this question and examine women I've worked with or encountered. They have shared their examples and stories, and they have inspired me. I have interviewed them, and I am sharing their experiences and wisdom with you. You will see that having it all for each of them means different things, and you will get to explore how they are choosing different routes at different stages of their lives. You will see that some of them are in their early twenties, and some are raising young families. You'll notice that they're always focusing towards the final legacies that they hope to leave behind.

I encourage you to see if you have the mind-set of, "I need to have it all. I need to have a great career, great marriage, wonderful relationships, etc." Ask yourself: "What are all those things coming together supposed to mean to me? What would they bring me? Does all this day-to-day business really result in bringing me those desires, or have I placed some assumptions behind those expectations that are not based on my reality?"

For example, you may tell me in a coaching session, "I need to be at the top of my company in order to have enough influence and earn a great living." Well, think about it. What does earning money for a great living mean to you? Would earning that money bring you that great living or the good life? Are there other ways to gain that lifestyle that might be less consuming, so that you have time and energy for other things?

I think *having it all* is a great expectation that the media, the stories we hear, and some of the role models that we have had instilled in us. It's not a bad thing to strive for, don't get me wrong, but its success relies upon the intention we bring to it.

What I'm saying is, think about *having it all* in the context of your life; in your legacy, what does having it all mean, and what would it bring you?

We need to clarify and filter it through what it means for us individually. Having it all means having the finances, stability, and relationships—and working all of those life pieces out in a manner that brings fulfillment. Then, the fruits of our hands will truly be blessed.

Women face many myths in life. When I was so-called "growing up" in the workplace (and even now when I work with the younger people as they graduate from school and are going into the workplace), the first myth I heard about women is that *once we have children, we are less committed—or we are perceived to be less committed—to our work.* When we have that assumption going into our careers, we may push back the idea of marriage and starting a family if we also want to advance in our careers. That might be good for some, but for many, it creates a struggle. That's also the time when companies are looking at lifting up leaders and giving them exposure and all the benefits that go with it. The demands of work may compete with a woman's desire to start or focus on her family.

Women may find themselves short changed, or feel that they are short changed if they start a family in this phase of their careers. Those in the workplace may assume that women with families are less committed because they are balancing a caregiving role.

I think it's a myth that women can't balance both, and yet it's often the thought in the minds of both the women and the company leaders and employees. But having worked with many smart and progressive companies in the last couple of years, I see that they are realizing that there is an issue, and they know their cultural assumption; they are working towards creating more supportive places for women who want to have children and pursue their careers on normal timescales and/ or longer horizons. These smart leaders know that women constitute a talent pool that they would love to have.

Women themselves are realizing, too, that they don't need to have this internal tension or dilemma over "career versus family" decisions. There are ways to work flexibly and contribute while also awakening to the fact that women can think about both their careers and families on a broader horizon. They are realizing that they don't have to compete with a man of the same age group, because the roles and responsibilities are different—and the way that women achieve fulfillment and happiness is different.

Studies have shown that the things that women feel fulfilled and happy about are different than those of men. As women, if we stop comparing ourselves with one another and with our male colleagues, we realize that the concept that women or moms are inherently less committed about their careers is a big myth. If we think about our career success in the context of a longer horizon, and we consider what brings us happiness and fulfillment—including what having it all means—the idea that women lag behind in achievement becomes a myth that should be busted from our assumptions.

It's time to change the mindset about women and career. We can pull from so many examples illustrating that when you change that mindset—when you eliminate that myth about being less committed and think creatively of how you can design your work, workspace, and professional relationships around *having it all* on a longer horizon—it can be done.

The second big myth that I see in the workplace is that *women aren't naturally great leaders.* They may be seen as too collaborative. They might be deemed as too soft. Or, women may tend to overcompensate and become what others might term as being *very aggressive* in the workplace.

How can we be happy and fulfilled in our authentic selves if we are pretending to be someone else? Our natural response might not include aggression; but that's what we think the workplace calls for, so there is a myth about needing to take on a different personality or persona to be a successful leader.

That's a big myth that is being broken down right now on a daily basis by many, many intelligent women who are influencing the workplace just by being their authentic selves. They are in total control. They are not living other people's lives. Instead, by being true to their own identities, they are living their legacies. They are choosing how they want to be remembered and what kind of relationships they want to have.

In being an authentic leader and one who is creatively expressing herself—carefully and consciously designing her leadership legacy in the workplace—the 24-Hour Woman is leaving a mark of having it all. She is illuminating the path of what a female leader can do, and showing how she can influence a bigger arena.

Angela Ahrendts, the CEO of Burberry, an iconic British luxury clothing brand, says in her post on LinkedIn, "Why a Successful Transition is a Great Legacy," that in her leadership role, her legacy is to ensure that she creates a smooth transition for the person succeeding her. That is her legacy—and her greatest satisfaction.

There are definitely many myths in the workplace. Choose how to respond to each of them so that your authentic self can come through, because in expressing yourself and knowing what steers you towards your legacy, you will find fulfillment and happiness—and probably less stress in the workplace.

Generally, I think there is also a sense that women are harder on one another, because we feel that we are the flag bearers; therefore, we need to lead the way and hold the standards. But I think there is a different and very real reason why there are fewer women in senior leadership roles in the typical corporate scenario. The typical age when companies tend to shortlist and develop high potentials for the leadership bench tends to fall around the same time women are considering marriage and child bearing. Many women resign themselves, saying, "I can't have the leadership role." Or, the lack of a supportive environment, network, or role models and mentors who serve in leadership positions may cause some to say, "I don't think I will succeed." There are also those who say very deliberately, "That's just not me."

However, in the emerging context, women are realizing that they can influence every level and that there are more role models and mentors available. There's a greater awareness and appreciation of what the role of a mentor or supervisor can do to help nurture and grow other women or men. So, for example, we are seeing more women networks. In those networks, it's not just about finding a business opportunity; it's also about helping others grow in their roles and responsibilities.

In the workplace, we are seeing more structured processes; but it is still a very competitive environment for women. Perhaps this is because, in the workplace, there are still very limited, so-called vertical career paths, and women today are not just competing against male colleagues, but also *with other female colleagues.*

If organizations in this very volatile, uncertain, and more complex world find ways to become more flexible, then I think they will create more room for collaboration. They will create space for women to excel, because women are a key piece in the puzzle of true collaboration. It's hardwired into us to look out for one another and help one another. I think as the workplace adapts to be more open and collaborative, women will rise up—not just to nurture other women—but also to help all of their team members or colleagues.

I think that myths about women needing to be "hardened" and needing to hold other women to even higher standards than others will eventually give way as the workplace becomes more open and collaborative—and being our authentic selves becomes accepted as a value rather than dismissed as odd.

As I reflect on my own life and journey, it was really in my late thirties that I eventually stepped into my own space and started to think about what I wanted. We would never have our present if not for our past, and part of the process of growing into a 24-Hour Woman involves letting time help us discover who we are and what we truly love. From the time that we are young children, there are already influences in our lives, and they are a little bit difficult to undo if we are not conscious about them.

"Sometimes I succeed, sometimes I fail,
but every day is a clean slate and a fresh opportunity."
—**Gretchen Rubin**, The Happiness Project

Ten Steps to Flexibility and Freedom at Work

One of the reasons the 24-Hour Woman can thrive in the world of work is because work has evolved over the years. Many roles now allow some form of flexibility. Even in the most challenging situations, if we exercise our creativity, we often can design a form of work that is flexible for optimizing our work-life balance. That's the experience my students and I have had since I began my practice in the work-life arena—and since I started my consulting practice around creating work-life strategies for companies (www.LifeWorkz.asia). This is also what I encounter and help people implement in the "Navigating Work-Life" program.

The shape of work is changing rapidly. It's getting easier and easier for people to work when and where they want. Over the past ten years, I've helped companies re-structure jobs so that employees have more control, flexibility, and freedom. **Here are ten steps, which I've distilled in the process of all of my work in this area, to get you on your way to flexibility and freedom:**

1. **Ask yourself: which type of work flexibility is right for you and your team?** When I studied companies that were successful at leveraging work-life flexibility, I discovered that there were at least seven different, most popular, common options offered by companies designed around place, time, and workload. For example, in a manufacturing plant operator role that's on 24/7,

try a different shift pattern or flexi-load. For a role that is not place specific, try telecommuting, flexi-load, or staggered hours.

2. **Talk to your manager and suggest an alternative schedule or work setup as a "pilot study" or for a "trial period."**

3. **Offer a proposed trial duration for the proposed flexibility.**

4. **Outline the roles and tasks you'll be responsible for and when you'll do them.**

5. **Describe how this flexibility will benefit the company or organization.**

6. **Explain how this flexibility will continue to support the company's business goals.**

7. **Address any changes that may happen as a result of the new arrangement.**

8. **Put together a communications plan and describe when and how often you'll be in touch.**

9. **Figure out the estimated cost of any new equipment (if needed).**

10. **Outline an evaluation plan—which means come up with a way that you and your supervisor can measure the success of the trial period.**

Now, as you can see, on one hand these steps are fairly self-explanatory. But on the other hand, there are many deeper layers to them. Visit www.NavigatingWork-Life.com for more resources

---

Putting It Into Practice

Irene worked as an administrator in a very fast paced and dynamic industry. She wanted to spend more time honing her craft in pottery, and she knew also that this hobby helped nourish her well-being. In turn, it helped her to be more productive and less stressed. Unfortunately, the classes she wanted to attend were only available on Tuesday and Thursday afternoons. She took the following steps in thinking through her proposal before approaching her supervisor for a discussion:

- **Which type of work flexibility is right for you and your team?** Irene noted all of her roles and deliverables and created a list dividing the ones she needed to do in the office from others that she would do offsite. She designed a way where she could work in the office on Mondays, Wednesdays, and Fridays for full days. Tuesday and Thursdays, she would telecommute and complete her other work in her own time and place.
- **Talk to your manager and suggest an alternative schedule or work setup as a "pilot study" or for a "trial period."** She worked out the schedule and confirmed her performance measures as she suggested a pilot study to her supervisor.
- **Offer a proposed trial for the proposed flexibility.** She proposed a three month pilot as her pottery classes were offered in a term of three months.
- **Outline the roles and tasks you'll be responsible for and when you'll do them.** She outlined her deliverables and responsibilities and how she would continue to be a dependable contributor to the team.
- **Describe how this flexibility will benefit the company or organization.** She cited case studies and her own experience to show how the flexibility would add value in terms of productivity and engagement within the business.

- **Explain how this flexibility will continue to support the company's business goals.** As there were no changes to her deliverables, one of her key focuses was on ensuring continued delivery of her key performance indicators and confidence from her team members—so they would continue to feel supported by her.

- **Address any changes that may happen as a result of the new arrangement.** Irene highlighted that she understood that on the days she was away, the team would need to reach out to her in different ways. She expressed her appreciation and was open to working with her team to find the best ways to ensure the workflow functioned for all.

- **Put together a communications plan and describe when and how often you'll be in touch.** After the discussion with her teammates, the communication and workflow was documented for all so that each knew the when, where, and hows.

- **Figure out the estimated cost of any new equipment (if needed).** No additional costs were incurred as Irene was able to use her existing work notebook for the telecommuting days.

- **Outline an evaluation plan—which means come up with a way that you and your supervisor can measure the success of the trial period.** No change was made in the way her key performance indicators were evaluated; but jointly, Irene and her supervisor decided that there should be team effectiveness feedback to spotlight potential improvement areas in supporting the team where needed.

Think about the various options possible for your role. Exploring the options gives you the ability to propose some form of flexibility when you need it to meet the challenge of being a vibrant 24-Hour Woman.

That's one of my desires in this book—that the younger generations will begin to keep open minds as to who they are, what matters to them, and what their life passions are, so that they can begin to pursue those things much earlier. But having said that, this doesn't mean that the act of pursuing their passions early in life would bring them the same level of happiness and fulfillment as finding it through their life paths. I think that there is great value in the passing of time. You discover yourself— who you are and what you believe about yourself—*and that takes time.*

In the current context, it's true that many of us come into our own spaces as women in our late thirties, and into our forties, because we have gone through perhaps three or four different career changes. We are into perhaps our second or third life stage, and we are grown up. We then know what would make us really fulfilled. If you look at choosing what to study in school, for example, very often we follow just what our peers are doing. Or we follow where the money is. How often or how many of us break the mold and follow where our hearts lead us at that early stage of life?

Designing Towards a Vibrant and Fulfilled Life— Building Towards Your Legacy

The first step is really to ask yourself, *what makes you smile at the end of the day?* I think the value of journaling and reflection is so understated. Journaling brings rich discoveries about yourself, your goals, and what you want to leave behind. The first step towards creating a powerful life legacy is to take time to reflect on a daily basis. *What makes you smile today and why?* Because as you gather that information about yourself, you will come to a conclusion about what you value and what's important to you—and you will begin to notice what efforts and areas bring you the greatest satisfaction.

Then, the bigger question after that is, *how do I monetize that?* Because chances are, you still need to make a living and work around your passions in the current economy and the current state of your role and job. *What things can you offer in terms of your knowledge and your skills that will be more satisfying?* There are platforms that allow you to search out such opportunities, so make the best use of them.

In the previous generation, this sort of exploration and change was much less possible. We were so structured to do a certain type of work in a very particular way. But now there are many more opportunities.

So to review, the first piece of assessing your life for whether you have tapped into your most optimal opportunities is to reflect upon what you value most and what matters most to you at the end of the day. Think in terms of your legacy, and then ask how you can monetize it. You may not have an immediate answer, solution, or path. However, this does not give you the permission to say, "I don't know what I want to do, and therefore I will do nothing."

Success comes through experimenting, and through that journey, finding out more about yourself so that you are able to determine what you want to be doing. Sometimes, this process points us to our natural strengths. You like to sew, or you possess a natural tendency towards working with your hands or researching. Those realizations give you ideas, but even those clues open you up to areas that are still very huge fields. Ask yourself: *What kind of research do I love to do? How can I monetize that? What kind of work environment do I seek? What kind of lifestyle would I like to apply my work to?*

I have friends who transitioned from working about sixteen hours a day, to working four hours a day. Their change was deliberate, because they had discovered a lot about themselves. They were able to ask, "How would I like my day to look?" and then search for work that would fit the kind of lives they desired. In that sense, they were determining what having it all meant for them, while not forgetting to determine how it might fit into their greater legacies.

The starting point to becoming a 24-Hour Woman is knowing enough about *you*. Discover yourself—and it can come through journaling, being open to doing different things, and learning what you love to do and don't love to do. Then, determine how to work around these factors. After you answer those questions, ask yourself: *How would I like my day-to-day to be? How would I like my year to be? If I were to imagine what having it all means to me and what that might bring, what would that look like?* Then, look for the different pieces—perhaps within your health, career or business, family or relationships—look for the things that bring it to fruition.

This is life, and therefore it evolves. There are no set pieces for you to play, other than your beliefs in who you are and what you seek in your own legacy. That's it, isn't it? The starting point, the end of the journey, and everything else evolves from that place of understanding what you stand for and what you most want to reach to achieve.

Now, regarding your journey and its ending place, if you do not know yourself well enough, you might be going up the wrong mountain. You won't find your fulfillment or legacy on someone else's mountain. You must make it your own.

Thinking about what really matters most to you is something you must do continuously as you evolve. The parameters for what is most important to you very seldom change, but through the years, you fine-tune those parameters.

During different stages in your life, you may think that you're shooting at different things, but at the end of the day, you'll find that you actually are looking towards achieving the same things—but through different means. I know I've said this, but I can't stress it enough: I strongly encourage you to start journaling every day to say *what made you smile, what made you fulfilled, and what made you feel that time was well spent.* Then, as you collect that data, look at how you can monetize it—leveraging from your knowledge and your skills. Ask yourself: *How do I move on from here if there are gaps in terms of systems, in terms of simplifying, in terms of the networks, or in terms of the people who can help me? Do I need to learn other stuff to get this done?*

Those questions are stepping-stones. But make sure they are stepping-stones to somewhere you want to go. Be very clear as you start out. Where do you want to head? Keep asking yourself until you figure it out, so that you remain intentional in your journey. For example, I worked with a young lady who said, "I know as I step into the investment banking world, I will not see the light of day for the next three years; but I am going into it with my eyes wide open, because at the end of three years, I will have sufficient contacts. I know, too, that I will have sufficient finances to be doing XYZ in this deep, social community space. That is what I want to be building my legacy up to be." She made short-term sacrifices to her ideal work situation in order to achieve her long-term legacy.

At your current life stage, you may feel that you have no time for anything else except work. So again, having it all doesn't mean having it all right now. It might mean having it all on a longer horizon; this woman clearly had her mind focused on a longer horizon. Her attitude said, "I'm investing in this right now, and it's hard; but I know that the pay-off will come in time. It will give me the ability to do a lot more."

I believe that our legacies will be refined continuously through the years with layers of experience, discoveries about ourselves, and steps we take towards getting there. In this process of achieving our legacies, we must take the first step to establish a foundation of *appreciation, awareness, and accepting.*

If we make a mistake and become aware of it, we *must accept that this might have been a misstep. We must tell ourselves, "Let's erase it and start again."* Success will come when we can accept the path we have taken, and build from our mistakes. Accepting accountability and a willingness to take action—forward—is a crucial step for the 24-Hour Woman. The "enemy" is not always *out there.* Sometimes the enemy is merely inside of us—in our heads—and then the mission becomes to seek a way to evolve and start again.

As we consciously design, there is an element of trial and error. There is an element of due consideration. There is an element of perceiving what's excellent, or what is good. Therefore, do not beat yourself up if you find that you're going down the wrong path. What should you do? Well, if you realize it's the wrong path, that's progress; you have a strong sense of awareness! Accept that it is perhaps not the wisest thing to continue on that path. Exercise accountability and take action to correct your cause, and then get back into the groove.

For me, I know from example in my different career changes that at some point I decided *this is not the kind of work lifestyle I like.* I might love it while I'm in it, but I ask myself: *Am I going to do this long term? Is it helping me to achieve what I want?* The truth of the matter is, in my early years, I had a very vague idea of my legacy; but as I grew up and as life unfolded, it taught me different things. While learning from other women and people in my life, I began to refine what my legacy was, and I'm still refining that to gain greater clarity.

Once we know that we aren't where we're supposed to be, we can course correct. Course correcting allows us to refine our paths and be even more conscious about the choices we make. That's the beauty of living our own lives; we are able to refine our paths, which opens so many choices before us. Then, we truly may enjoy our journeys as 24-Hour Women. *We just have to know consciously what our choices are, what each might bring for us—and where we are heading.*

The 24-Hour Woman Speaks
Ms. Evelyn Kwek (Singapore)
Director, ThYnk Consulting

Evelyn Kwek is the director of ThYnk Consulting. Evelyn is a 24-Hour Woman whose life is centered around her family and career—and juggling the two, while also having time for herself. If we look closely at her story, we will see how she has applied the five Foundational Pillars to her life to create a *life most excellent.*

When Evelyn first started her career, she worked for the Local Tax Authority as a tax collector and then eventually transitioned to the HR department where she got to help many people. She remembers her senior boss once stated that HR was a calling, which stuck with Evelyn. She realized early in her career that she enjoyed meaningful relationships and really wanted to help people. Evelyn possessed an immense appreciation of where she was in life. She appreciated that she had a great job that offered her the opportunity to work with people and make a difference. She was happy and knew that something was working for her.

After five years of working in HR, Evelyn quit her job for a year to move with her family, because her husband's job had relocated him. Most women would view this as a step back in their careers, but Evelyn made good use of the time and brushed up on her skills. She was very aware of her situation and understood that she could easily fall behind in her career.

Instead of falling below the mark, Evelyn accepted the terms of her situation and used her time wisely. She knew it would be easy to lose a year in her career, but she accepted that things were okay. She had resources and awareness of her situation, which enabled her to take action.

Evelyn kept in touch with colleagues and people in her workplace, and continued to read and expand her knowledge of the HR field.

In preparation for jobs in Taiwan and the Taiwanese Chinese environments, she bought textbooks in Chinese on HR and learned many of the HR terms in Chinese. Evelyn explained that learning those terms really helped her, because doing so exposed her linguistic abilities to prospective employers. The reading of Chinese text helped her to develop that new skill. When she finally came back to the consulting firm, the fact that she knew technical terms in Mandarin set her apart from her competitors and helped her achieve new goals in regards to the projects she undertook.

These positive aspects in her life were a direct result of her awareness and acceptance of her situation, which then moved her to take action. Evelyn was able to use those skills to advance her career to her current position as the director of ThYnk Consulting—which she is passionate about. Evelyn now engages in meaningful work and changes the lives of those she works with. Evelyn said in our interview:

> *I think we are very motivated to want to create great workplaces for people. We didn't want to just do projects, come and go, but we really wanted to, like what I said earlier, touch lives and make a difference. Whether we work with leaders, or we work with employees, or we work with the strategy piece, it is about doing meaningful work, doing work that leaves a legacy that's sustainable.*

Evelyn also shared her inspiration, struggles, and motivators that have helped lead her to a successful and fulfilling life and career. When asked to define success, she said she thinks of success as doing work that adds value and makes a difference in people's lives. But it is also important to her that she not only has success in her career, but also in the other core areas of her life such as family, friends, health, stability, and meaningful relationships.

Evelyn discussed how outside factors also allow her to create a *life most excellent*. She describes how her tribe of people all help to make her life successful:

> *I think you are first a woman, then a mother—not a mother, then a woman. I really believe in finding that balance. I've also been very fortunate to have a great network of support. I've had great parents in-law, great parents who are able to jump in anytime I need, great friends who live in the neighborhood, and we do car-pooling. It's a wonderful idea, and that really helps; we jump in for people. When they are busy, I jump in; when I'm busy, they jump in. These are resources that I lean upon and depend upon to help me to feel fulfilled and to live this life.*

Evelyn shared what she hopes will be her legacy, which she is constantly working towards. She would like for her friends, family, and girls to pass on her understanding of what living a fulfilling life is like. She wants the people in her life to think that she has done something positive to affect lives around her. In the area of business, she at least would like to be able to work with companies to transform them, even if it's just one workplace where people think that it's because of the work that ThYnk has done, the company has improved.

On a final, closing thought, Evelyn expressed her thoughts about the growing opportunities for women:

> *I think more and more women are becoming educated. We are very independent minded. I've seen a lot more women at a very young age who are choosing to step out of a full-time career to be more hands-on to raise their families. I would like to see more women thinking beyond raising their own families, even if that*

does sound politically incorrect. While it is very important, and I totally believe in it, I'd also like to see how we can leverage off our skill sets to go beyond our families, because I think that we have given so much through our education system, throughout the economy, that we definitely have the capacity and ability to go beyond raising our families, to our community. Many mommies would set up their businesses. I just want women to think bigger and to think beyond kids and family, because there's so much more we can do.

As you read these interviews from women around the world, you will notice that the cultural expectations and norms vary. In some cultures, staying home with children is more "the norm" than in other countries. But throughout these interviews, you can gain glimpses into some of the common threads that these women use to weave the tapestry of their legacies.

Want to watch the full interview? Come on over to www.The24HourWoman.com/blog. Share with me your comments, and ask your questions. I would love to hear from you.

Taking It Home: Three Steps to Wrap Around Your Schedules

As a working professional or entrepreneur, you still are called to wear different hats and probably have many things happening at the same time. How do you keep track, and how do you decide which to attend to? Our aim is not just to complete our to-do lists. In fact, it's not about the to-do lists. It's about doing things that are directed towards building the vibrant and fulfilled lives we desire. One of the key challenges many of my students face is keeping track of events—from meetings to holidays to meet-the-teachers sessions in school to medical appointments for our parents. I know that at times I have forgotten an appointment or double booked myself.

Here are three steps that have worked for me and the busy 24-Hour Women I work with: (You may also download the checklist and planning chart for this at www.The24HourWoman.com/Resources)

1. **At the beginning of the year, decide what are the important things you want to accomplish that will build towards the vibrant and fulfilled life you desire.** This becomes your filter as to what gets on the schedule or not, and in what priority. For example, I love to use the rule of *what I will do more of and less of* as one way to decide which important and meaningful tasks and projects get space in my calendar.
2. **Keep all activities in ONE calendar that you keep at hand.** You will realize the insanity of keeping multiple calendars and trying to reconcile them. It doesn't work.
3. **Categorize.** (I like to use color codes.) Enter the activities into the corresponding categories as much as possible—business/work, family events, children or elderly parents' events, personal (facials, gym, ME time).

Regardless of whether you are using a digital calendar or a pen and paper "war sheet," use the tools that work best for you. I like to see an overview and then break it down to month, week, and day—which means, yes, I have a fairly elaborate planner—but that's just me.

What other tips or ideas do you have regarding managing or organizing your schedule effectively? Email me at solutions@The24HourWoman.com. I would love to hear your ideas, and I am sure you will inspire and encourage others.

The 24-Hour Woman Signpost for Chapter 3

It's time to uncover and discover your assumptions and recalibrate. Consider these questions as you reflect on Chapter 3:

1. What does having it all look like to you? Why are you striving to have it all?
2. What myths have you adopted about thriving and having it all as a 24-Hour Woman?
3. What is the legacy that you want to leave behind?

Chapter 4

THE BIG IDEA

"Give her of the fruit of her hands;
and let her own works praise her in the gates."
—Proverbs 31:31

his is a beautiful quote from the Bible: "Give her the fruit of her hands; and let her own works praise her in the gates." It is found in Proverbs 31, and it means a lot to me, because for me, it is a blueprint of the best role that I believe I can have as a happy and fulfilled woman. This chapter in Proverbs talks about all of the different facets of our lives. It talks about relationship with a spouse. It talks about business, if you can imagine it. It talks about how to weigh the different goods, and talks about how to bring what we have created—like our knowledge and skills—to the marketplace.

It also talks about how to take care of family. It discusses that the lights never go off. The family and the people in your life—not just your immediate family, but the people around your household—remain cared for. Proverbs 31 has always been very close to my heart, and this is the last verse of the entire chapter. I see it as a sort of legacy, the conclusion of a powerful book of the Bible that is touted and quoted in many circles and walks of life.

As we live our lives, and especially in our twilight years, the fruits of our hands are blossoms. There are good fruits—and they might not be just our bank accounts, but rather the lives we have touched. The fruit also exists in the friendships we have built and the health we have. "Let her own works praise her in the gates" means to me that as we journey through life, the things we have produced will turn into praise unto us and an appreciation back to us. We don't need to look towards ourselves for fulfillment or beat ourselves up for our inadequacies.

For me, "give her of the fruit of her hands" is really about how we journey towards our legacies, and at the end point, what matters most to us is what truly impacted us; the sense of appreciation and praise comes from these different sources we have tapped into and the results we have achieved. I think that being able to reflect back on life in this way and experience the abundance of a *life well lived* is a beautiful testament of a life that is *most excellent*.

You've probably heard about the seven key areas of life for the 24-Hour Woman in many different forms and formats. I've distilled them into this structure because it made the most sense to the women that we have worked with over the years; and it made a lot of sense to me.

Seven Focus Areas of Life for the 24-Hour Woman

The seven key areas, that, when woven, form the tapestry of the 24-Hour Woman's life, are:

1. Family
2. Relationships
3. Work or Business
4. Health
5. Community
6. Beliefs
7. Self Renewal—ME Time

You'll find that these are core, and some feed off others at different life stages. These seven areas might appear differently at every stage in life. We can always go back and renew and adjust. There are some things that might be key at one time, while others are not.

For example, the importance and role of family changes over time. At this moment, perhaps you are single, but it doesn't mean that you have no family responsibilities. You might have dependent care responsibilities in terms of an elderly adult or parent who you care for. When we talk about family in this discussion, therefore, it's not just about children. It's also about your relationship with your partner or spouse, siblings, parents, or whoever touches your life in a close and intimate way.

For me, *family* is foundational. It is a key unit that we come back to, regardless of what the storm is like out there. It is a crucial piece that we need to ensure we care for. But *relationships* outside of family are important, too. We invest in our "growth friends"—those who help shape us on our journey. We invest in relationships with our team members and the people we work with, or the receptionist we see as we walk through the office, or even the person we see when we get into a taxi cab.

Do you express thanks to those you encounter—for example, the taxi driver? You can appreciate that there's a taxi to drive you. You can appreciate that the driver decided to stop and pick you up. Little behaviors like that help make others' days, and also help make your day, because you are practicing a very foundational step of showing appreciation and gratitude. Those actions will, when practiced often, become habits to you.

The third area that is key to fulfillment as a 24-Hour Woman is *work and business*. By that, I do not exclude stay-at-home moms or stay-at-home caregivers, because I am very impressed by mothers or individuals who decide to stay at home and look after the household; it is a lot of work. I have known of so many women who decided, *I'm going out to find a job rather than work at home, because this is a lot of work that very often goes unappreciated.*

When I talk about work and business, it includes stay-at-home moms, because their contribution is as much; they are looking after the next generation, or even the last generation. They have to be even more conscious about setting time and boundaries and making sure that they create a focus on the family, on their relationships, and on their own health.

The next point about health for all of us globally is that in regards to our physical bodies, by and large, in recent years, we tend to be sleeping less. Most of us are getting by with five or six and a half hours of slumber. We think we can get away with this diminished rest, but our bodies do not gain sufficient time to repair themselves. Do the symptoms show up instantly? Even if not, they will show up later. For some, they show up the next day—either as eye bags or an impaired thinking and decision making ability because we did not have enough rest and can't think clearly. Your brain is not well rested, and your body is not well rested.

We interviewed one CEO who used to be a workaholic. He used to work for sixteen or twenty hours a day, and said, "Oh, I can survive with four hours of sleep." Then, there came an occasion when he realized that he was lacking sufficient rest over a period of time, and he knew that his sense of awareness, alertness, and decision making had been impaired by staying up for late night calls and answering all of the devices that he had when they started beeping. He realized that *if that's happening to me, what about these other people whose sleep and sleeping patterns I have been disturbing?* He began to advocate that they receive sufficient rest.

Arianna Huffington of *The Huffington Post* also realized the price one could pay due to exhaustion. When experiencing that type of sleep deprivation, we fall well outside the realm of wellness. When I talk about the importance of retaining our health, I'm talking about our overall well-being. Sometimes, for stay-at-home moms, health is the thing that we compromise first. For those of us who work outside the home or run our own businesses, it's also a place where we compromise, because we don't see the immediate effects of not taking care of our health until much later. Sometimes, correcting a health issue after it becomes a problem is a lot more challenging than being proactive about it.

A *community* is one of the key components to the 24-Hour Woman. We need to realize that we live in a space that extends beyond just ourselves and our family unit. There is a bigger community into which we need to have a sense of grounding. But many times, in the modern world, we don't even know our neighbors because we are so busy; and that becomes a symbol of our failure to build meaningful community relationships. For those of us who do not stay near family, our communities are our source of help and support; so reach out and get to know your community and build those bridges.

Beliefs are another important component to the 24-Hour Woman. I think this is an area that we often keep in the back of our minds—not letting it surface until we are in trouble or caught in a crisis. Then, it shows up out of desperation. I think for us to invest proactively—I say invest because the rewards that we have from this investment are a lot more than just tangible, because they help us discover more and more about ourselves—it helps us build resilience within ourselves, which is very essential as times get challenging. We dig deeply within ourselves, and if we do not fill the space with these resources, then we find ourselves running on empty when we most need help. There is nothing there for us to hold onto when we need it.

The last key component to the 24-Hour Woman is *life renewal*. I put it in last place deliberately, and you might not find it at all in other models you've seen. This is because people forget that renewal is about themselves, in terms of deliberately finding time to refocus and realign. It's an opportunity for us to refresh and consciously look at life to ask, "Hmm, maybe this is the wrong cause; how can I course correct?" Setting time aside for that review process is important. Similarly, setting time aside for renewal in terms of self-maintenance and being able to, for example, schedule an annual medical checkup, is also important.

You might scrutinize and place scheduling of an appointment under health; and true, health matters should be on an everyday calendar. I will climb twenty flights of steps, ten times a day. That's about health, right? But renewal includes not things that we do on a daily basis, but those that come occasionally or quarterly. We need to make time for these actions. We need to schedule them in. Another example of renewal, in my own life, is scheduling some time with my husband and family every thirty days just by taking the weekend off.

Renewal can also happen at the end of every single week. For me, it involves taking some time off just to be; and when I say take time off, it means take time off—no headphones, no emails, and no television. I become tech unplugged, to spend renewal time from the distractions, so that I also can experience really deep renewal and connection with people. The strength of those relationships means the most to me.

What does renewal mean to you? Because at the end of renewal sessions, you should find that your well-being has been enhanced. They should give you a fresh burst of enthusiasm and energy—a sense of being ready again for the work at hand. I feel that in a world that is 24/7, taking time to experience a sense of renewal is critical. If you want to avoid being burned out and experiencing your relationships breaking down, you need to consciously focus on bringing a sense of renewal into your routine.

Technology: a Friend or a Slave Driver?

The 24-Hour Woman makes the best use of technology, but she is not a slave to it. That means knowing how to leverage technology to your advantage in the seven areas, and be able to, at the same time, set boundaries around using technology. Think of us having a conversation right now. It's evening for you, but it's morning for me. You could actually set boundaries to say, "I can't do calls any day that might be during family time, but I can do them on Mondays and Wednesdays. The rest of the time, I need to reserve time for my family."

When I travel, I will Skype or FaceTime with my children, so I make great use of technology in that sense. That keeps connectivity. With my teammates, in terms of work, we make a lot of use of technology, because my team is global. They are all over the world. There's no way that we can all go to a shared space except for maybe two or three times per year, but the rest of the time, we work virtually.

Technology has enabled work to be done in new, innovative ways. Again, rethink; technology can enable the busy 24-Hour Woman to complete her work in a much more creative way, which might not have been possible in the past. New technology has enabled her to work with team members in the remotest parts of the world.

Technology is not just restricted to the workplace, but is also used within the family unit. Cooking is a lot faster now because of modern technology; instead of using old hand tools, I now use a blender. Some older folks may claim that the food tastes different, but what's important to me is that I cook a nice, warm meal. I enjoy the process of cooking, and I enjoy serving a warm meal to my family. The technology in the kitchen has enabled me to do that, rather than slave over pounding spices. Another piece of technology in the kitchen that I utilize is the coffee maker.

I love, love, love that technology is there. But remember, technology should help make our lives better, and if technology is not doing that, consider setting boundaries. In her book, *Hands Free Mama*, Rachel set her boundaries very clearly around why she wanted to unplug technology, and when she would do so. I've seen many, many high performing individuals, both men and women, who decide that "these are my boundaries as far as technology is concerned," and the boundaries work to create better balance for them. When they answer emails, when they answer Facebook posts, when they answer the phone, they do so during predetermined times. These technology tools do not interrupt their workflow or their days, because they have set a predetermined time when they will check in with those items. Consider setting these boundaries for yourself—and consider altogether unplugging yourself at least once per week from technology. Doing so helps you to reconnect with yourself and the people around you.

One final piece about technology: now that we have the Internet and streaming of movies so freely available, we can and do engage in them through watching films and gaming through the night with competitors. That's happening around the globe, and it has actually taken a toll in terms of health and building relationships. We have heard so many horrifying stories about people who are so engrossed in playing games that they forget that they have not fed their children, for example. Or they have not slept for three days, and they literally burn out.

We also have heard of women who have been so caught up with Korean or American dramas that they just get sucked into them as a lifestyle. It's an indulgence. Yes, you can use these technologies, but be mindful of their effect. They are supposed to help make our lives better, and not make our lives more stressful by eroding our relationships or quality time for work or community building.

The Time Is Now

I truly hope that people will not wait for a time of crisis to begin consciously designing their lives; but the truth is that it's often our wake-up calls that get us to make changes, isn't it? My advice is to take a step back from where you are today—before a crisis hits. Be more proactive. Most of us do our planning, for example, once a year—and usually towards the end of the year. My advice is to plan every quarter. If you were to take regular time for renewal—and take time to re-look and reassess—where would you be?

Ask yourself: *Are your relationships where you want them to be? Is your work or business where you want it to be? How have you been nourishing yourself in terms of your beliefs?* Build those habits on a quarterly and even daily basis so that you hopefully avoid the crisis as a wake-up call.

But sometimes it does take a crisis to wake us up. For example, a really high achieving woman who spends 80 percent of her time traveling because it's part of her job, and has two young kids, came back one day and realized that her child had a cut and was in pain. Her child ran towards her helper rather than her mother. In that moment, the woman's heart sank, because she realized, "My god, what legacy am I leaving here for my children?"

She realized that she didn't need the level of financial affluence her job was bringing her, and that became a wake-up call for her. She loved what she did, however, and gained a lot of fulfillment through her career. So she negotiated for a lesser role that would still leverage on her skills but reduce her need to travel as much. As a result, she became much more involved in her children's lives. She got to know them and built those relationships once again.

Not all of us have that luxury to downsize our careers or positions, because we still need to be working. I'm not saying that you can or should stop working. I'm saying: *do what you love to do. What are your knowledge and skills? What do you value most? Go back to the fundamentals and say, "Okay, this is what I can offer; how can I monetize that?"*

Here is a quick exercise for you to create a snapshot of where you are today. On a scale of 1 to 10, what is your state of engagement with each of these seven areas at this season in your life:

- Family
- Relationships
- Work or Business
- Health
- Community
- Beliefs
- Self Renewal?

On a scale of 1 to 10, where would you like the state of engagement of these seven areas to be, where 1 means *least needed* at this season in life and 10 means *most needed* at this season in your life:

- Family
- Relationships
- Work or Business
- Health
- Community
- Beliefs
- Self Renewal?

Keeping your legacy in perspective, and knowing where you are at this season in life, ask yourself: *Where are the gaps? What can you do to shift towards living a vibrant, joyful, and fulfilled life?*

Try creating a great story about appreciation and a sense of awareness about where you are, and accept that you need to do something about this. Then, begin to look at what your knowledge and skills are, and explore how you can transition to a different road that allows you to begin evolving towards living a life that you find more fulfilling—while building a legacy that's more meaningful to you.

Five Practices to Effectively Manage a Diverse Team

As demographic shifts become more apparent and irreversible, one of the stresses at work/business is managing an increasingly diverse talent pool. As a contemporary leader at work or in business, you need new skills and perspectives. One question I'm often asked is, "What do I do with my team whose members are so distinct from a culture, gender, and generation perspective?"

Here are five practices that have worked for the participants from my "Optimizing Generations at Work" and "The Contemporary Leader" programs:

1. **Trust and respect all hands on deck.**
2. **Harness the differences by cultivating a platform that values diversity—and manage that diversity towards a specific outcome.**
3. **Leverage on the commonality this builds—through common ground and bonds.**
4. **Manage a workforce of ONE.** Yes, you will have policies and practices, but how do you convey and make them meaningful to that *one* team member?

5. **Treasure your gems across culture, gender, and generations.** We know there is a talent shortage. One of the ways to engage and treasure your gems is to play to their strengths. It's how it works for us, too. If we are given a task in which we know for sure we will succeed, would we not want to do well? Think about it. If we overlay the task with a bit of a stretch, the challenge and novelty will push us internally just a little more.

Putting It Into Practice

Here's how Esther, who was managing in the financial sector, applied her learning to optimize her diverse team.

- **Trust and respect all hands on deck.** Esther practices public praise and private correction because she believes that fundamentally we all have the innate desire to excel.
- **Harness the differences by cultivating a platform that values diversity, and manage that diversity towards a specific outcome.** She allows the voice of even the quietest team member to be heard regardless of whether she is the youngest or the only one who telecommutes or is from a different culture. She does not stop there. She then has the rest of her team members build on that person's idea so as to benefit from the different perspectives, ideas, and energies of the group.
- **Leverage on the commonality this builds—through common ground and bonds.** Esther, through her interactions with her team members, discovered common areas of belief amongst them. They all believed that their organization's products and services were great, for

example; hence, she rallied them behind the products and services so that their work as a team became stronger in service of their clients.

- **Managing a workforce of ONE. Yes, you will have policies and practices, but how do you convey and make them meaningful to that one team member?** Having a diverse team and making work meaningful for each and every team member might seem unfair, because there may be an expectation that "if my boss can allow *her* to come in for only two days, she will let me do the same thing." But your role might not permit that sort of flexibility. The philosophy is to practice flexibility, but the way it is implemented for each staff member may be different. Esther decided that, philosophically, she would practice the policies as defined—but make them practical to each of her members.

- **Treasure your gems across culture, gender, and generations.** Esther expresses her appreciation explicitly in ways that encourage the hearts of her team members.

Appreciate your diverse team and increasingly diverse customer base. How else have you engaged your diverse team members? I would love to hear your stories.

Let's explore two different approaches to evolving towards living a life that you find more fulfilling. One, *become regular about your review and reflection over what matters most, as you discover more about yourself.* Two, *become deliberate in building towards that legacy in areas where you already have clarity.* That's what the 24-Hour Woman should be doing—consciously designing every moment that she has a choice in influencing. If, unfortunately, a crisis causes you to wake up—whether it's a health scare or a relationship loss, alarms have gone off—take time to unpack everything and repack it again in a way that helps you to live a more fulfilled and happy life in the context of the seven areas that we discussed in this chapter.

That opportunity to change, I feel, is still a blessing. It beats waiting until the end of your life and then realizing, "Hey, what happened? Why didn't I...?" Don't live in regret, but live in aspiration, with ambition and the awareness that you can create the pathway to your legacy.

In fact, if you look again at Proverbs 31, the pathway, *the model*, is there. How do we interpret that in modern society? What does that mean, and what does that mean to me, when it says, "Give her of the fruits of her hands; and let her own works praise in her gifts"?

What does that mean to you? By using the gifts we were given, I think we can consciously design the lives that fulfill us. Along the way, as a particular piece of learning hits home with us, we have the opportunity to redesign our lives to make them *most excellent*.

☀ ☀ ☀

"Being Hands Free matters. Before, I was holding on to the wrong things and missing out on life. Finally, I am holding on to what matters, and it has given my life new meaning. Grasp what really matters to you and then start living."
—**Rachel Macy Stafford**, www.HandsFreeMama.com

☀ ☀ ☀

Taking It Home: Five Ways to Parent with Grace

As a working mom, I find many stresses and challenges while parenting in this busy and media intense world. One question I have been asked frequently is *how can I love my children in this busy and complex world?*

I am in the process of raising three boys who were born between five and six years apart. I have experienced raising a child from baby to teenager, along with his two younger brothers. Any older, and he will be a young adult, which would indicate a new and different relationship between us built upon the foundation of the earlier years. Having read parenting books that resonate with my values and beliefs, and developed my own strategies along the way, here are my five tips on parenting with grace:

1. **Be present.** How true is the saying that the greatest gift our children need from us is not the presents we buy them—but that we are present when we are with them. Do set boundaries and establish routines that you will do with your children or with each child.

2. **Talk to them without judgment.** Here's what I typically talk with them about: *what's happening in their daily lives, how are their friends, what are their opinions about XXXX?* Let them talk without making judgments or corrections. Still praise in public, but correct in private.

3. **Share with them your thoughts and opinions.** Take this opportunity to build values and speak life into them. We know that what we focus on expands. So give them a good foundation in terms of values.

4. **Take care of them—not just through the physical provision of food and shelter, but teach them about safety when interacting on the Internet, what they feed on via the media, and how to make sure they rest well.** That means providing proper meal plans, eating dinner together (when possible, daily), doing physical activities together (at the playground,

playing Frisbee, etc.) establishing routines and traditions, and having fun.

5. **I know that my God has the best plan for me and my children, and I will always repeat and bless them with that promise. Do this, too, if it works for you.**

Parenting is one of the greatest joys I have had the privilege of engaging in. My three boys have taught me so much about being a 24-Hour Woman and refining my legacy.

What are your thoughts about parenting with grace? Email me at solutions@The24HourWoman.com. I would love to hear your ideas, and I am sure you will inspire and encourage others.

The 24-Hour Woman Speaks
Hong-Ling Wee, PhD (Singapore, now in US)
Ceramics Artist

Dr. Hong Ling Wee was formerly a research fellow. Today, she is a ceramics artist. When asked how she got started, she states:

It was really serendipity. I was actually a science student all along. I was in the United States pursuing graduate studies. NASA funded my research. I was using satellite images to look back at earth to analyze environmental problems, the growth of cities encroaching upon our natural environment, deforestation, and so on. At the time, an American friend said to me, "Hong Ling, you are too focused on research. You should try to live a more balanced life, so how about trying something new and different?" and I said, "I don't have time for something new and different, I can hardly manage my time just doing the old and the same."

He did not take no for an answer and signed them up for a beginner's pottery class. "I was really reluctant to do that," she states, "But I went for my first class, and upon touching the material, everything shifted...I had never made things with my hands. I was very good at writing, I was very good on the computer, but now, to turn a ball of clay into an object, that's a completely new experience for me."

She explains that it was like learning a new language. "I was terrible at it," states Dr. Wee. "I didn't have the vocabulary or the skills, but what drove me was the passion for it. I just fell in love and wanted to do more and more of it." She spent more time at the studio and less time at the research lab. Time passed, and her skills in ceramics improved. She also slowly managed to finish her research. At the crossing point in 2005, she finished her graduate degree and went from being a researcher to a ceramic artist overnight.

It was a huge switch for me, because I think that having always been trained in the sciences, you are trained to collect information, make very rational decisions about things, do data analysis, and stuff like that. All of a sudden, you have to switch gears, do something different. You have to create absolutely from nothing. That was really new for me. First, it was really scary, not knowing how to approach that field or go about doing those things for which I had never been trained or went to school for. But, I think that my science background was very helpful in my establishing the arts career. There is not enough said about being organized, having good reasoning skills, having good management skills. Even though all I needed to manage was myself, I didn't have a team to manage, but yet those things all came into play and those were, I think, my strengths, and really helped me in establishing myself as an artist.

Dr. Wee explains that the biggest challenge in this transition was not knowing where to start. "When I decided to become an artist, I had already established a full resume as a scientist," she said. "So when I looked at the artist resume that was blank, there was nothing. How do you begin all over again after you have spent your whole life establishing your identity?"

That's a question many of us ask ourselves as 24-Hour Women, and probably one of the reasons why many of us hold back. We establish ourselves so much in one area that it seems impossible to abandon it for something else—even if it is more in line with our legacy.

Dr. Wee said that in order to make this leap, she had to be very honest with herself and ask, "What is it that I want to do?" She realized that in the mornings when she got up, she could not wait to go into the studio and create a piece of work. "Even though I was very good at research and what I did, I never once jumped out of bed to go into the lab to turn on all the computers." She decided she wanted to give the best years of her life with an able body to do the work she loved. She was not willing to go in half time as a hobby, because she did not feel that she'd find the time to pursue it while working sixty hours a week.

When asked what she would advise as a first step in considering a change to pursue a passion, Dr. Wee stated, "I think you first have to identify your fears. I think once you identify your fear, you can actually have better control over the situation. Not identifying your fear just allows your fears to control you." When she analyzed her fears, she realized she had nothing left to prove to herself. She simply was ready to pursue her passion.

Some stop pursuing their passions due to the fear of rejection, she explained. What if people say, "Really, this is what you make? Are you sure you want to be a full-time artist? You're not really good enough." There are conversations like these in our heads, she explained. But for her, it was more important to try. She realized that a fear of rejection was from the outside. She told herself, "As long as I have done my best, and I am fulfilled in what I do, then the other things are pretty secondary." That pushed her forward.

Dr. Wee has spent a fair number of years away from Singapore, in New York. When asked how she balances her work and non-work needs and her family back in Singapore, she stated:

Thank goodness for the Internet. We are all global citizens these days. You are never too far away. You can easily hop on a plane and go home. Yes, New York is half the world away, but I can be home in twenty-four hours. I try to make about two trips a year if I can. I have a lot of ties in Singapore. The thing is, you try to identify what is most important to you, and when you do, you can always manage it. Time is about prioritization. If it is important enough, you will find the time to do it.

Thirteen years later, she still can't wait to get to the studio. "When I am actually creating my work, it's timeless." Still, she works in time to do other things, such as research about other arts that inspire her, visit the museum, and see people she cares about.

Dr. Wee was recently granted an award for outstanding contribution to community environment by the Society of Foreign Consuls (representing one hundred, ninety-six countries) in conjunction with International Women's Day.

I am just so thrilled that I get to do the work that I do, and it actually has this impact on community, that what I am doing is empowering others to choose the life they love and pursue their passion. It doesn't really matter what people are interested in. Of course, my primary material is clay, but this translates into everything else. If I can speak with someone who has a vague interest in furniture design or fashion or poetry or anything for that matter, it is to encourage others to really grab the bull by the horns, go for it, and do it.

She adds, "We don't have to be interested and passionate about everything. If you say no to everything, then do you ever find it? Try to say a yes to some things at least; being open may guide you to something you like."

To those starting out, she heeds these words of wisdom:

Just be brave enough. Because we are so trained in what we do, we are very good in that, and to suddenly be exposed to something that we don't know how to do, that is frightening. But don't be afraid. When you find the thing you are passionate about, the thing you cannot wait to get up and do, do it really, really well. Do it like your life depends on it. It is in doing that you will be surprised where that will take you and how you may be rewarded.

Through her travels to Tibet and elsewhere, Dr. Wee says:

I think my work is always about creating houses, a sense of belonging. I think that comes from being away from Singapore for twenty years and my search for something to anchor. Houses are very easy to relate to. Everyone can identify and relate to it as structure of comfort, security, community, friendship, and kinship.

Want to watch the entire interview? Visit www.The24HourWoman. com/blog. Share your thoughts. I would love to hear from you.

Signpost for Chapter 4

You've guessed it. It's time to journal. Now, consider these questions as you reflect on Chapter 4:

1. Keeping your legacy in perspective and where you are at this season in life, where are the gaps?
2. What can you do to shift towards living a vibrant, joyful, and fulfilled life?
3. How can you better manage your energy, instead of just your time, so that you are very targeted in where you invest yourself?

Chapter 5

THE FIVE PILLARS OF THE 24-HOUR WOMAN

"A cord of three is not easily broken."
–Ecclesiastes 4:12

*A*s I've worked globally with women and examined my own life experiences, I've discovered and uncovered five key foundations or Pillars of the 24-Hour Woman. Remember, we are talking about the woman who thrives in work/business and life—and has an ongoing sense of fulfillment and happiness.

In order to truly embody what it means to be a 24-Hour Woman, it is important that we become aware of and embed these foundations into our daily lives. The five Pillars are:

- **Appreciation,**
- **Awareness,**
- **Acceptance,**
- **Accountability,** and
- **Action.**

Let's take a deep dive into each of these and discover what they are all about, where we stand in achieving them, and how we might amplify the areas where we are already AWESOME and learn new habits to enhance the areas that need more attention.

Before we start, perhaps our best method for moving forward is first to stop and look at ourselves in the mirror. Yes, we may not see a nice picture; but if we each face our reflections with courage, we can make progress going forward. *Why waste time and energy going around in circles again?*

Appreciation

The first Pillar is a reflective one wherein the 24-Hour Woman *appreciates* where she is—identifying the growth that she has achieved over the years while recognizing the opportunity to grow further. She appreciates what she has—no matter the amount. She appreciates her overall situation, and that ability to appreciate starts from knowing that she isn't starting from ground zero. Some things already have been working for her. When she can see her progress and the positivity that has come from it, she is starting from a position of strength and thankfulness.

Status Check

On a scale of 1 to 10—wherein 1 means you take a lot for granted and 10 means you are fully aware and count your blessings constantly— *how appreciative are you of the following: what you have, where you are now in life, and how blessed you are in your workplace, family, and other areas of life?*

Closing the Gap

Between 8 and 10: Great job! But you know, it's only the beginning. *Continue to cultivate an attitude of appreciation and gratitude.*

Between 5 and 7: Good start with some foundation and sensitivity towards being aware of blessings in your life and demonstrating that gratitude and appreciation. *Continue to journal as these positive points in your life are treasures that you can store up. Be ready to extend your appreciation through words and deeds—making sure that those deeds encourage and touch the heart.*

Between 1 and 4: *Take note and take stock of people, situations, and things that are looking up for you already. Take proactive steps to appreciate the beauty and awe of what you have. Start from a position of strength. Begin to journal at the end of the day, and be thankful.*

Awareness

The second important Pillar of the 24-Hour Woman is awareness. She holds keen awareness of what's happening around her, and *to* her. She is aware of where she is and where she wants to be. She is aware of her enablers—and what might be in her way of progress. She is very self-aware of her legacy and very involved in creating her own definition of success—even if it is a work in progress.

Status Check

Again, on a scale of 1 to 10, *where do you live day-to-day? Are you unaware of your direction (or season) in life? Or are you moving forward towards a 10—being totally aware of your passion, purpose, and how you can prosper in your legacy?*

Closing the Gap

Between 8 and 10: Self-awareness is one of your greatest assets. An inflated ego is of use to no one. Keep your sense of awareness sharp— not to reprimand yourself, but to course correct where needed.

Between 5 and 7: You have some sense of direction, even as you are trying to navigate around the bends. You are in the process of refining your purpose/legacy and plans to get there. The more aware you become, the greater your refinement and confidence.

Between 1 and 4: This is the time to dig deep within to know yourself—who you are, and even more so, who you want to be. *What drives your passion and purpose? How can the various pieces of your life fall into place to create an intentional picture?*

Suggestions to Close the Gap

Following are three suggestions to help you tighten the gap between where you might be today and where you wish to go tomorrow. Remember, pick those tips and tools that you are comfortable keeping. It will take time to peel through the "onion" to get to the core. Yes you are like an "onion." There are many intricate layers to the real you. It's important to be committed in this discovery adventure.

1. **Journal what you are thankful for at the end of each day.** Go beyond the physical object and situations into the deep areas of feelings, emotions, and the non-tangibles like friendships, parenting, and community engagement.

2. **Ask yourself periodically what makes you smile.** What makes you come alive? What engages you? What makes you tell yourself, "That's tough, but so worthwhile."

3. **Define your legacy.** This one will take some time to refine, particularly if you are not very self-aware. Some say it comes with age. I say it comes with experiencing life; then you know

what really matters! So at your eighty-fifth birthday, beyond the candles, *what do you hope to have achieved or built towards?*

Acceptance

The third Pillar of the 24-Hour Woman is a sense of *acceptance* for the reality of where she is. It means acknowledging the situation as it is—without denial or accusations. A 24-Hour Woman acknowledges her status and moves on accordingly. She knows what she needs to do. She is able to say, "There's no blame. I take accountability and responsibility." She also knows that the biggest enemy is not always the one found "out there." Sometimes, the real enemy is her own sense of denial—or her limiting or wrong beliefs. A 24-Hour Woman accepts what was in the past and what's in the present—and moves forward.

Status Check

Again, rate yourself on a scale of 1 to 10, wherein 1 is burying your head in the sand of denial over what is unfolding or has happened, and 10 means rationally and emotionally accepting what's going on so that there is closure (or at least an acknowledgment so that you can do something about it). If you do not ever acknowledge the situation, how can you take action towards it?

Closing the Gap

Between 8 and 10: You have a high sense of "taking it all in." *Good for you, but be careful not to beat yourself or put yourself down. A healthy dose of knowing who you are is important so that your self-esteem lies in good standing. You will know what's needed to bounce back when you encounter difficulty.*

Between 5 and 7: You have a nice sense of acknowledging what's happening. There might be things beyond our control. This is why it's called life. *Take it in stride and move on. Develop a sense of humor.*

Sometimes we need a good laugh over a situation so that we can just move on.

Between 1 and 4: No good will come out of denial. Not seeing reality does not mean it's not there or happening. I learned from personal experience that the longer one is in this state of deception, the tougher it is to face the issue head on. *So do yourself a favor: acknowledge the situation or outcome rationally, but do not take it so personally that it breaks you.*

Accountability

The fourth Pillar of the 24-Hour Woman is *accountability*, and that means amending and correcting whatever has happened. The 24-Hour Woman has the discipline to do more or less of whatever needs to be done in order to journey towards her legacy.

Status Check

Again, rank your life's events on a scale of 1 to 10, wherein 1 means that you feel *the negative things that happen to me are always the fault of something or someone else*, and 10 means that you can rationally say, "That is my mess up; I take responsibility and will tweak or refine towards my legacy." Doing so requires that you align your desire, direction, dedication, and choices in order to make constructive decisions.

Closing the Gap

Between 8 and 10: It's nice that you are taking responsibility. *Be careful not to assume more responsibility than you should; not all things should be borne by you or are your responsibility to solve.*

Between 5 and 7: You possess a strong sense of responsibility and accountability. *Be certain to direct your sense of accountability upwards towards constructive behaviors and a positive outlook.*

Between 1 and 4: *Take a step back and reflect on times when you have had a hand on your life's outcome. There is no point in crying over spilled milk. Take heart, and take responsibility for what has happened at home, work, and in the rest of life. Learn and grow from your journey—one step at a time.*

Action

The fifth Pillar of the 24-Hour Woman is *action*. This Pillar comes with a caveat: taking action does not mean striving and driving until you burn out. Taking action means engaging in the behaviors that you strategically know will bring the necessary results to achieve your legacy or goals. This also means admitting that in some cases, doing nothing is the course of action needed.

Status Check

Again, rank yourself on a scale of 1 to 10, wherein 1 means you over plan, over think, or procrastinate, and 10 means you always are doing or prone to take action.

Closing the Gap

Between 8 and 10: Very nicely done, busy bee. *Just make sure you are busy and productive towards the legacy you are building and not taking action just because you need to be doing things. Sometimes it's necessary, in fact deadly, to just go on and on and on. (This may lead to burn-out, exhaustion, disappointment, or running the wrong race—or someone else's race).*

Between 5 and 7: You are responsible and accountable for what needs to be done. *Make sure that you are responsible for the things that matter most to your legacy—and not driven by an arbitrary to-do list.*

Between 1 and 4: *Plan sufficiently (most would say to follow the 80/20 rule, wherein you lay out 80 percent of your plan up front and let the other*

20 percent reveal itself as you execute), and then evolve. You will not have the perfect plan, especially as you first begin to make plans; but you can have a great ending—if you start, learn, and evolve. You don't have to have perfection to start. The most important action is just to start!

That's it! Those are the five Pillars of a 24-Hour Woman: a sense of *appreciation, awareness, acceptance, accountability,* and *action.*

How Does It Work?

One way to develop a sense of gratitude and appreciation of our blessings, the strength that we have, and what is already working for us, is found in our ability to say *thank you* to those who have supported us. Appreciation may reside deep within our inner person; but the ability to express it engages the external self to make it a part of our personality. Actively demonstrating a sense of appreciation for somebody or a situation is the first step towards implanting this foundational Pillar into solid ground.

The act of appreciating a situation takes away the negative aspects of that situation. It's impossible to focus on what you are grateful for in the exact same moment that you complain. Sometimes it is with a bit of humor that you can say, "Hey, I don't know why it happened, but I appreciate that it happened. There's something to learn from the situation, and that was a great laugh to be had." Being able to appreciate things which were none of your doing has a great influence on your attitude. Your sense of gratitude and appreciation, and your ability to see things in a positive light, affects how you will respond to life. This becomes the attitude with which you combat negativity.

Why don't we just pick a posture of appreciation—rather than a posture of defense—and move on? For example, if my five-year-old cried over something or just wanted my attention, and I was not able to give him my attention at that moment, should I snap at him—or should I just hold him and say, "Hey, I appreciate that you want to talk to me. I'd love to make conversation with you, but first I need to finish this email. Then, I'll be right with you."? Showing your appreciation for your child's needs prevents you from feeling defensive or guilty with thoughts like: "Oh, I'm not looking after my child. I'm actually looking after my emails. I'm not a suitable parent!" All it takes to make this moment work for you is just a demonstration of your appreciation.

This example also demonstrates the value in having a sense of awareness of what's truly happening around you. We discussed the big picture in regards to being aware of your past and present and where you want to go in the future. This kind of awareness gives you the strategy and big pieces that form the basis for your life. But in regards to day-to-day living, awareness applies even in the smaller moments.

Becoming aware of how you will design your conscious responses will affect the outcome of your relationships. I know many people who say, "Oh, it's so tiring to have that level of awareness. I would have to be so conscious while having those conversations on a regular basis." But as you create a habit around your consciousness, you'll discover the mindset that you need to have. As you build the habit, it will become second nature to you, and then it will not be so laborious. When you consciously design your responses, and you're aware and develop those habits, you create the "you" that you want to be. You undoubtedly will feel satisfied and happy that you are a better person—or that you have grown up to be someone that you would really like to be.

In the total picture of where you want your journey to go in terms of a legacy, accept that in this stage of life, some things might not be possible. But that realization shouldn't stop you from taking steps in the direction of your goals. Try finding other ways to contribute to your desired legacy or direction. Try accepting that your kids may be still toddlers, or that mobility might be an issue for your career right now, but that shouldn't stop you from asking for assignments that might take you away for a day or two, for example. Even if you are bound to your home office for now, you also still can gain global experience. Or try asking for assignments wherein you will work with a virtual team; you will be exposed to working with people of different experiences and cultures.

At some point, things undoubtedly won't play out as you thought they would. Let's say mobility is high on your list of desired traits in a job, but right now, you need to stay close to home to care for young children or an aging parent. Look at why you feel that you need that mobility. Why do you feel that you need to relocate? When you know the answers to your "why" questions, are there other ways to get around them? Awareness arrives when you know *the why*. When you accept that your reason for wanting mobility is that "the traditional way of getting the task done is *so* not for me at this point in time," it allows you to look at how else you can achieve a similar outcome or emotion. If experiencing a diverse workforce is the true "why" behind the desire to be mobile, for example, there are other solutions—such as working on a diverse, remote team.

Having this "why" discussion with yourself gives you a way to achieve what you desire despite current restraints; but it also tests your creativity and puts the control back in your hands. Rather than just saying, "There's nothing I can do about it," you have a sense of clarity on what the objective is. You can ask yourself: "How can I achieve the desired experience in a non-traditional way?"

In many companies where I have worked, there have not been detailed solutions handed out, but people have stepped up and become innovative—taking joint responsibility—and in doing so, were able to work out even more powerful solutions together. If there was no acceptable solution, they had the awareness to say that there might be a limitation. If you accept reality, the control is back in your hands, and then you can ask, "Now what can I do about it?"

I deliberately placed action as the final Pillar, because we all have huge to-do lists that don't end. The question is, "What action would be strategic enough to 'move the needle,' or change things, for you?" Take *those* actions. Taking action isn't about being busy for the sake of being busy. Instead, action in the sense of the 24-Hour Woman means making sure that the big pieces are in place to move us towards where we want to go. Taking action towards those goals through your daily behaviors and through consciously designing what's happening in the different areas of your life will ensure that you end up moving towards the legacy that you're building.

But action without appreciation or awareness would be futile. Without a sense of acceptance, you start to put blame and accountability on others. Really, the opportunity for meaningful action lies in your hands. It's what you do with it that matters most. That's why action is the final Pillar, because it's not just about being busy; it's about directing your actions towards building something that will bring you fulfillment and happiness.

Five Ways to Create ME Time

In the midst of your busy day, how often do you stop *for yourself?* Do you give until you are so empty within and then realize you need to crash?

Why do we have no problem prioritizing other people's tasks or agenda for us, but we don't build ME time into our daily, weekly, monthly, quarterly, and yearly plans?

ME time does not just happen on its own. Everyone from your home, business, office, friends, and family may want a piece of you. However, it's worth the effort to carve out time for yourself to rejuvenate and reflect. **Here are the five ways I create ME time:**

1. **I block out key days that are meaningful for me**. This includes my birthday. Yes, most would want to celebrate with family and friends, but as I reached my mid-thirties, I began to value this

as my special day when I wanted to be by myself to reflect and enjoy my own company.

2. **I take a mini break every ninety days.** I first learned this from one of my mentors. I do this either with my spouse, with one or all three of my boys, or with a group of my close girl friends. We just unplug from work/business and indulge in other things. Each time, I return with renewed energy and enthusiasm and a greater sense of creativity—having been reconnected to self and seeing things with a different pair of eyes. Block out time to try this. Know that work will always be there and is never really all done, so you have to work around your responsibilities to create time just to be yourself.

3. **Bundle activities together so that you can take advantage of the time you have more fully.** For example, I like to read or listen to podcasts when on public transport. I listen to non-work-related topics—such as fashion, the arts, design, or something that connects me to my creative side. Another similar strategy to wind down is to watch favorite television shows while working out on gym equipment.

4. **I strategically say no.** The biggest key for me in setting up ME time is found in saying NO to people. This sometimes means I am saying no to my children, parents, or spouse— which is hard to do. I have resorted to hanging a sign on my door (or telling others): "Building ME in progress." And I tell my kids, "Mommy needs some time—like you get when you play by yourself with your own toys or read your own books." I tend to have at least thirty minutes of ME "sanity" time daily. Sometimes, it comes just by having a walk in the daylight!

5. **My best ME time happens when I do my daily devotion, as it sets the tone for my day or night as I rest.** (see Putting It Into Practice sidebar).

Putting It Into Practice

Let's explore how you can create your own ME time:

- **Practice block-out time days/weeks/months in advance.** As one who advocates having everything in one calendar, it is most useful when you can use red to block off breaks—including a time of day, day of the week, and longer mini-time-off every ninety days. If you can see your schedule at a glance in the calendar, you also can see the rhythm of developments and where you can come up for "air." Document how you respond to your time off once it's done. In the beginning, as you start to carve out time for yourself, you could be reluctant to break away. I want you to document the renewal or sense of new perspective you have when you return, so that you will gain confidence in granting yourself permission for these breaks.

- **Bundle.** Look through your tasks from the past four weeks. What activities can you bundle together so that you can gain some self-nourishment while getting other things done?

- **Practice saying no gently but firmly.** Some may not understand why you need ME time. Offer them alternatives to whatever you have been asked to do—or let them know when you will respond or do things with them.

- **Connect with yourself each day.** Reaffirm and keep the big picture in mind.

Make a list of all possibilities, and experiment with them to create time and space that nourishes you.

How About a Final "A" to Top It Off?

How about A for *Awesome*? A sense of celebration helps to reinforce your efforts. Recall the quote that we spoke about in the previous chapter: "Give her of the fruit of her hands; and let her own words praise her in the gates." It's a quote of celebration. It's a quote of joy. That's actually how a *vibrant, joyful life most excellent* should be expressed.

It is one thing to give thanks, but another to celebrate! Convert your joy and sense of fulfillment into an external expression for yourself and others.

Integrating a sense of accomplishment and fulfillment becomes our reminder—a record of our milestone in our journey and development—and the signpost of the fulfilled and happy 24-Hour Woman.

"Being a mom comes in really handy in running a business. I always tell my children, 'You've got to look at your glass as half full, not half empty.' So, I remind them, 'When disappointments happen, look at your glass as half full.' I ask them what other things are going right in their lives, and then maybe the obstacles or the disappointments are a little bit easier to take. And I think this applies to global business. If you are focusing on all the problems that need attention in the developed part of the world, you are looking at your glass as half empty. But we've also got to keep encouraging people to look at the glass as half full. And the glass that's half full is the upside potential and opportunity that there is in Asia and the Asia-Pacific region."

–**Deb Henretta**, Group President, Global Beauty, Procter and Gamble (*View*, "Interview with P&G's Asia Group President Deb Henretta," Issue 15. December 3, 2013)

Taking It Home: Three Ways to Build Meaningful Traditions

One of the ways to bring meaning and build a legacy in the family or community is through creating and keeping traditions. When I say *traditions*, I do not mean just following mindlessly what has always been done. Each tradition should serve as a joyful and meaningful foundational stone—building deeper relationships or stronger purpose.

One of the key challenges I initially met was to identify what was worth having a tradition around, and why. Then, I put practices into place in these areas. Some of my traditions came from my upbringing in a Chinese family. As you build your traditions, make sure that they fulfill your desires for family and community. Here are three of mine:

1. **Ensuring that the family spends Sunday dinners together.** It's guarded and protected. In most scenarios, we say "no" to appointments or dinners with others in favor of spending time with our family. If your family is not living in the same city, where this is possible, then make it happen every quarter or during every holiday or festival that the family celebrates.

2. **Keeping an item from each of my boys' childhood, so that they have an item to pass on to their children.** A hardy, non-toxic, painted wooden walking duck; a stuffed toy caterpillar called Cleaver; a set of shape sorters made of wood—these are all the toys that will help our family members pass along valuable memories and traditions to one another. You may ask, "What will the children do with them? They might just throw them away." But if we explain with love how each item was chosen, talk with each about how he enjoyed playing with it, and describe how it communicates the love of the giver and of the person who has played with it, meaning is built behind the gift. Yes, it take time and effort to build meaning into the item

and process, but it's a valuable way to pass along feelings of love and belonging.

3. **Taking a personal trip with each child when he turns six.** Formal education begins at seven in Singapore, hence my husband and I decided that we would take a holiday with each of our boys when they were six. We wanted to spend time *just with that boy.* We have been going to Disneyland since we took our firstborn there when he was six. This trip now serves as a milestone and sort of coming of age for the toddler as he becomes a young boy.

You may download a list of traditions to consider at www. The24HourWoman.com/Resources.

What other tips or ideas do you have regarding developing traditions for your family or community? Email me at solutions@ The24HourWoman.com. I would love to hear your ideas, and I am sure you will inspire and encourage others.

The 24-Hour Woman Speaks
Susan Chong (Singapore)
CEO, Greenpac

Susan Chong, founder of Greenpac Singapore Private Limited, is a 24-Hour Woman. Despite it being a very male-dominated field, Susan recognized a problem with the amount of waste her country was producing, and entered the business of sustainability.

Susan's passion for sustainability started earlier in her career when she was working with her husband in the packaging industry. Because of that job, Susan saw firsthand how much the industry was wasting and decided to do something about it. Susan said: "I was actually helping my husband in the packaging industry, where I saw there was a lot of waste.

As I travelled the world, I also realized that packaging actually creates a lot of waste. That's why I wanted to do something to reduce the waste and do it in a sustainable way. That's how I got the idea and started it."

Similar to the other 24-Hour Women, Susan used the five Foundational Pillars to leverage her strengths and create a *life most excellent*. Susan was very appreciative of where she was in life. Although she knew she had a rough road ahead of her, she also knew that she wasn't starting from scratch. She appreciated the skills she had and knew they would apply to her end goal.

Susan was also very aware of her position. She knew that getting into the field of sustainability was going to be difficult, because it was a new concept in Singapore, and it was also a male-dominated field.

She accepted her position as a woman in this field and took accountability for how she would control the way people would accept her. She knew that starting a company around sustainability would be difficult, but also knew that the end result would lie in her hands.

Susan took action in 2002 and started a small company that she believed would give her access to a *life most excellent*. She said in our interview:

> I think at that point in time, a lot people didn't take it very seriously when you tell them "sustainable." Big word, good, but what is that for me, right? Nobody will actually buy the idea. I actually spent many years, in fact the first few years of our business, educating and sharing with people "what is sustainable all about"? I think that importantly is how do we do that in a sustainable way and achieve bottom-line cost saving? I think that's what people are interested in—the bottom-line cost saving—and it's small and sustainable.

Susan used her knowledge of sustainability to educate people, but she also knew that people didn't just want to know about the idea of sustainability; they wanted to know what it would do for them, particularly in the amount of money it could save them. So she did just that: educated them on how being sustainable could save them money.

This strategy of educating her clients quickly gave Susan the respect she needed. Susan grew the company organically without investors, and simply added staff when she needed to. She started with just three positions in the company and now has grown the company over the years to have many more employees—most of them women. Susan said:

> *I think, as a woman, you have a better opportunity, because they'll respect you once they know that you are capable. You get some special treatment occasionally, especially in a male-dominated industry. That's always good and bad, but so long as you establish yourself, people know that you really mean it. If you actually show what you can contribute, people give you the respect.*

Susan slowly grew her company, and because of the business model she presented, customers knew her value and what her company could bring them in terms of financial profits. Some of the customers were even willing to give Susan cash to fund the projects together, and that's how they grew—organically.

When asked how Susan copes with juggling family life and her business, she said it is always very challenging.

> *For business, it's not difficult, but as a mother juggling all the time, that is the challenge. My work requires me to travel a lot because a lot of the deals are struck at the corporate level, so I have to travel to meet people. My traveling schedule is typically to fly into the US, the next day have the meeting, and then take the next flight*

out so that I can get everything done within the week. At least I still have my weekend with the kids. Of course, my mother-in-law has been living with me. She is a great help with the chores and all that. Of course, we have a domestic helper. The kids grow up well, and they are very independent, I think, because of the environment. Of course, for me, it's always a struggle. You try to do a lot in the workplace, but you kind of also worry that you neglect the family when you try to do so. Constantly, you just have to strike the balance. It's not easy.

In some cultures, having a mother-in-law living within the home would not be the norm—or perhaps even desired. But for Susan, it worked well—as it does for many other women. As we've discussed, there may be different tactics used by many of the 24-Hour Women highlighted in this book, but many of the issues and overall strategies for managing work-life have value to *all* women. The important thing is not that you follow any one tactic outlined in these examples, but rather that you see the essence of how women have adapted to manage their challenges while reaching for their legacies.

Susan manages her life by seeing the patterns that present themselves and trying to manage a schedule that is equally beneficial for her business and children. She says it's the hardest part of owning a business.

Susan has a strong drive to push her company to where she wants it to be, and she is very motivated in this arena. When asked about handling her multiple roles and which role means the most to her, Susan replied:

I guess I'm in the business of sustainability. That's something that is really close to my heart—and also corporate service responsibility. So when I founded the company, that's always the thing that came into my mind. I want to do good—do well and do good at the same time. Because it's reality. You know, you can do good, but if you don't do well, it gets you nowhere. But when you do well, you want to do good at the same time. I try to incorporate those kind of values in the company as well. As for my legacy, this world doesn't belong to us; it belongs to our next generations and what you really want for your children. We try to create a better place, so for them, in the time to come, they can also enjoy it. We are only doing the very bit that we can do to contribute to society so that we can conserve the environment for the next generation.

Susan's dream in terms of her legacy is what provides her with a *life most excellent.* Although the odds were stacked against her when starting this company, she knew that sustainability was important to her. She used the five Foundational Pillars to shape her life and took action towards what she wanted. Now, she has a very successful company that is taking strides towards making a better future for generations to come. Because of these actions, Susan is able to live a vibrant and fulfilled life.

Want to watch her full interview? Come on over to www. The24HourWoman.com/blog. Share with me your comments, and ask your questions. I would love to hear from you!

Signpost for Chapter 5

This is a critical piece in your journaling process. Consider these questions as you reflect on Chapter 5:

1. Review your status for the five Pillars of the 24-Hour Woman on a monthly basis through journaling. This allows you to gain solid, in-depth insights into how you are doing.
2. Read through and refine what you desire as a manifestation of the five Pillars to the 24-Hour Woman.

3. How have you been giving yourself permission to dream, evolve, and design your legacy? If not, what's in the way? Are the assumptions you hold valid?

Chapter 6

CASE STUDIES

"Life is not a dress rehearsal."
–Rose Tremain

Remember Esther?

*I*n Chapter 1, you met one of the ladies I worked with who we referred to as Esther. She is similar to the majority of the women I work with who are professionally trained, very successful in their careers, raising a young family, and usually from a two-income family. Esther was doing really hard work and expected to be promoted. Part of the promotion, however, involved agreeing to gain some global exposure. Mobility was going to be an issue. She was also managing a virtual team, so she was expected to be on call in different time zones even when she wasn't traveling.

One of the factors that she was overwhelmed with was how she could continue to do well at work while also being there for her children. Recall that instance when Esther's young child was injured and ran towards her caregiver rather than to her mother? It really broke Esther's heart. She was thinking, "I'm working so hard right now, and at the end of the day, it is my family who is paying the price." She was conflicted and wondered what to do.

When I started to work with Esther, we examined what we could do to solidify the five Pillars in her life. Esther openly expressed *appreciation* to her husband and her caregiver. She had an *awareness* that she needed to be more present with her child. Therefore, she began to design a specific block of time every day to spend time with him before he went to bed. She *accepted* that there were some restrictions in her life in terms of how frequently she could spend time with him and how that time would be spent. She also accepted that she needed to find a way to work around it.

After about two and a half months of working through her concerns and negotiating, Esther was able to put some strategies into *action*. She looked to her supervisor, and that's where she put *action* behind what she had learned in another one of our programs called "Navigating Work-Life." She learned how to approach her supervisor to ask for flexibility in her schedule and determine which phone calls would be mandatory to join.

Esther also began to look at how she could work differently with her virtual team. She tried empowering them a little more—just checking on their key milestones and deliverables—but not micro-managing them. She then began to carve out time to come home two hours earlier on certain days of the week to spend time with her child—going back to work again later in the day.

In terms of mobility, Esther negotiated for a role wherein she did not need to travel for extended periods of time. She did not need to be overseas over three-month periods or be stationed somewhere for a year or so. She began to look at how she could manage all of her employer's expectations and needs—and balance them with her own family and deeper life priorities.

She took short trips for exposure. Whenever she had to be away for a longer trip—such as a ten-day trip—she intensely covered a lot of ground so that she did not have to travel as often. She displayed the courage to negotiate so that she didn't have to be stationed away from home for a year, but she could take those shorter trips instead.

She still took *accountability* to say, "With these changes, I'm still comfortable with my role and feel responsible for my team, but also *accountable* so that I don't feel like I am depriving myself. I don't want to feel guilty about my relationship with my child." Then, after six months, we reviewed all the key indicators of what was important to her. It was all positive in terms of the team's response and engagement, and her output as a team leader. Her relationship with her husband and child actually improved, because Esther was more present. She was determined to be different, and she was able to manage her time differently—finding new ways to put the pieces together.

She'd also begun to simplify more. For example, regarding the number of calls she had to take each day, she was able to reduce it to only what was actually needed. She also looked at how to bundle different tasks together. Instead of conducting separate calls, some calls could be bundled together to be more efficient—getting everyone into a conference call at once. Instead of having a team call every week, Esther had them only on alternate weeks to give everyone time to ensure that the necessary work was completed. She practiced different strategies: **systemizing, simplifying, bundling, outsourcing, or alternating.** (See sidebar for more on these.) Through it all, she continued to be a contributing member to her organization.

Esther's story began on paper as she reflected and figured out her strategy in pieces at a time. Her story was also about her accountability and taking action. All in all, it took about six to nine months for Esther to get into her new rhythm.

Define, How to Apply, etc.

Here are some strategies to become more effective with your use of time and energy:

- **Systemizing:** Develop a set way to organize a practice or process. When you systemize on a consistent basis, you create habits so that the process becomes highly efficient when done well. A system also allows you to have a standard process to delegate or teach others. An example of this happens when you share a system with a teenager on how to tend the garden or sort out items to give to charity. Once he understands it, he can do it himself, and train others how to do it.

- **Simplifying:** This involves stripping down to the core of what really needs to be done to achieve a thriving and fulfilled life. Begin by journaling all that you are doing and how much time you spend doing it. Then, prioritize the list. Zoom in on, say, the most important "top fifty" activities. Draw a line below them and focus on prioritizing those fifty, because they are the most crucial to you. As you go through your list, ask yourself the big WHY—why should I do this, and am I the best person to do this? If not, simply outsource or delegate to someone else. If you can't answer a why, don't do it just for the sake of completing your to-do list. For example, do you really need to watch another, brand new, Korean drama after just completing one? Or would that time become more productive through reading with your elderly parent? Paring down is one of the most difficult things to do. But you can gain so much freedom and the "currency" of time when it's done right.

- **Bundling:** Some call this multi-tasking. Research has shown that multi-tasking is actually distracting and causes us to be less efficient. We have the perception that we are getting more done when we multi-task, but the opposite occurs. Bundling involves putting two complementary events together. For example, taking a walk to the grocery store to take in some fresh air and exercise—while buying healthy food to cook for dinner instead of driving to the shop—completes two needs at once. Other ideas include: Having tea with a friend rather than having tea alone. Or reading a book while you have tea so that you are nourishing yourself in more than one way.

- **Outsourcing:** This may involve using an external resource (which might incur some expense) or internal resource (called delegation). Setting performance measures and managing performance is most critical when outsourcing, as the other party may have a very different way of getting work done or defining the success of this outsourcing relationship. But doing so can also free up valuable time if done well. *What can you outsource?* Remember your list of fifty? Go through it again. Ask yourself as you go down the list: "Do I really need to do this? Can I delegate or outsource this to someone who might do an even better job?"

- **Alternating:** This time and resource saving tip involves having it all, but not at the same time—or all of the time.

You create a routine that changes on a set schedule. For example, this could mean going to the gym that is ten minutes away from your parents so that you can visit them before or after you exercise on "even" weeks, whereas on "odd" weeks, you may go for a run in the morning and catch a light breakfast with your growth friend(s) before heading back to work (we will discuss growth friends more in Chapters 7 and 8).

Putting It Into Practice

Let's explore how the tactics we've discussed in this chapter may apply for you. Take out your calendar and list all of your tasks, including the times you are engaged in these activities. Then, look at your top fifty list. Are those activities in your calendar? Are there items for ME time? Family? Work/business? Belief? If not, are there opportunities to put any of the time and resource saving tactics to use?

Some of the items that will make the greatest difference in our lives are not new. You may have done some of these things before. But the success will come in doing them consistently and mindfully. So pick a couple, leverage on the tactics, and enjoy. Remember, some of the "greats" of this world are successful because they put these tactics and strategies to use consistently.

Which of the time and resource saving tactics appeal most to you?

Here's Jen's Story

Jen's story is interesting because she is a baby boomer, and many of her kids are already grown up. Jen expressed, "I want to have a more vibrant life. I've been working for more than thirty years. What's next?" While she didn't actively explore other options, she did begin to ask herself, "What would I like my life to be like when I reach retirement?" She realized that retirement in the traditional sense wasn't such a viable or appealing option anymore. First, it would be difficult financially to retire, and second, it would be hard to stop her mind from wanting to do more, since it was still very active. (Many who are nearing retirement age share similar thoughts or situations.) So why wouldn't she want to create action in the form of a second career? She realized that she was still in a good enough state to do work that she loved in order to acquire an income, although she knew she did not want to work long hours. She wanted to pursue different work options that were more in line with her current desires. In her mind, as a baby boomer, there had been very little talk of the idea of transitioning to a second career. By the time my team began to work with her, she had begun to explore other work options—and also began to explore a possible corporate crossover to become an entrepreneur.

Jen sat down and looked at her situation and said, "A good part of my so-called adult life is behind me. My children are away in college, and they're thinking of themselves. What do I want as my legacy?" Jen began to realize that she needed to make the best use of her time. She redefined her legacy and began to work towards it. Initially, she was overwhelmed, thinking, "Oh my goodness, do I really have the time to make that change?" But as we worked together and broke it down, she eventually said, "Yes." Each step of the way, she found some bigger steps and smaller steps to travel, but she began making a difference each day.

Her legacy and life are still a work in progress, but she has applied the five Pillars of the 24-Hour Woman: *appreciation, awareness, acceptance, accountability*, and *action*. And they are working for her.

Five Ways to Keep Energized at Work

Have you ever felt like an ever-energized, little bunny all day—busy at work—while on other days, you just feel as deflated as a balloon? Well, there are things you can do to keep your energy up. As you become a 24-Hour Woman, you will realize that sustainability is greatly desired. One question I've often been asked is, "Cheryl, you have so much on your plate; how do you keep yourself energized?" Here's what I do. I practice these five tips and share them with my audiences in my programs:

1. **Keep your eye on the goal.** Keeping the big picture and how meaningful the goal is at the top of my mind has been particularly useful for me as I write this book. On days when I feel low in energy or down emotionally, I remind myself why I am writing: I desire for all *women to have access to a method for thriving in work/business and life.* This book provides access to those who might not be able to join me for an online or live experience. They are supported. That is what gets me up and enthused to get moving. What is/are your reason(s)? What is your big *why*?

2. **Brighten your environment.** I love flowers at work. They brighten the room, and when coupled with a nice, uplifting fragrance, they make getting things done so much more enjoyable. Also, don't underestimate the effect of music. Some of my best work is done to the songs of ABBA, the Beatles, Celine Dion, and Adele—while other times I work best with the consistent rhythms of the Baroque era. As some

of you might have guessed, sometimes I love to work in the quiet of the night—and other times in the buzz of the middle of a Starbucks.

3. **Track progress and movement.** One of the things that most energizes and motivates me is to see progress—to witness movement towards successfully completing what needs to be done. You would be energized by this, too; think of the joy experienced when placing a huge tick against your to-do list— moving you closer to your legacy.

4. **Foster physical and mental well-being.** Well-being extends beyond just wellness, and it is a more desirable state. Exercising regularly and managing our workload and habits will enable us to perform at a higher level over a sustained period of time. Consider it like owning a car; being in good, well maintained condition helps us perform better. Speaking of which, what you use as fuel makes a difference, too. There are many references about nutrition and eating well. Do your research, and discover what works for you.

   Our energy drops as we stay stationary—which happens when we work on our laptops or simply stay in a physical posture. We need to move our bodies every forty-five to sixty minutes to get our blood flowing. And we need to remember to breathe deeply on a regular basis as we tend to take shallow breaths when sitting down. This mental break also interrupts our thoughts and helps us take in our surroundings and gain new perspective. Certainly, if you are on a winning streak, however, then go with the flow until it is all done!

5. **Foster an optimistic outlook.** A positive attitude has carried me, and many of my students, through times when we were depleted. Let the buoyancy and joy of your hope in the future energize you.

Putting It Into Practice

Let's explore how you might be energized at work. Consider what you do at work. Here are some areas to consider:

- **Your mental game.** What does the little voice in your head tell you? How do you manage that voice for a positive outcome—so that even though you are physically spent, you are able to keep at it?
- **Your physical well-being.** Have you been exercising to gain both flexibility and stamina? What about watching what you consume? Are you consuming endless, zero value, fizzy drinks—or consuming foods that build you and infuse you with good fuel that will enable you to do what's necessary? Do you have friends who will nudge you along in the right direction?
- **Your environment.** Do what you can regarding your work environment within your sphere of influence. Decide: Do you work best with music, or not? What type of music, if so? What kind of physical environment charges you?

Take note throughout the day of what refuels you, excites you, and motivates you. Make a list of all possibilities, and then explore in more depth to define what works for you. As you explore, do not drift away from finding the activities that support your purpose, mindset, desired response, environment, or physical well-being.

Over to Sylvia

Let's revisit Sylvia. She was younger than twenty-five years old, and her life ahead of her was just *so exciting*. She realized while looking at her parents that there had to be more to life than just work. Her parents were both working when she was growing up, and she felt that surely there must be more to life. She asked herself, "What will my legacy be?"

Sylvia was still defining what strengths she could step on when we started to work with her on her legacy. Sylvia was young, but she had already thought that life fulfillment was not just about what action step to take, but also about discovering who she was and who she wanted to be. Defining a legacy *involves discovering who you want to be*, and that's the amazing piece that Sylvia worked to find.

Sylvia appreciated what her parents had done for her. She appreciated that she was born at a point in time when there were so many changes that allowed more opportunity for women than in past years; she was fully appreciative of that particular opportunity, and her part in it. She gained such an awareness of the wonderful opportunities available to her. She began exploring and discovering things about herself at her stage in life so that she could further apply them to defining her legacy.

So far in this book, we have talked not only about the five Foundational Pillars, but we've also asked you to explore the life stage you are in right now. *What strengths and awareness do you already have?*

As you see these women's stories unfold and how they make use of the Foundational Pillars in the different areas of their lives—whether it's work, finances, career, relationships, or a sense of belief—they all come together differently. The Pillars play out distinctly based on their different life stages and areas that they want to explore. Esther's story was very clear; it was about family, relationships, and her work and career. For Susan, the story was very much about her belief and self-discovery—and her legacy. For Jen, it was about career, belief, relationships—and renewal, because she believed that there was more to life than just the work she had seen her parents engage in when she was young.

Again, the five Foundational Pillars are at work in many diverse ways. These Pillars really frame how we fulfill and achieve our legacies— through the seven different areas of life with which we interact.

Our Beloved Abigail

Abigail, like most entrepreneurs, thought that we control our time, energy, and destiny when we become entrepreneurs. This is very true if, and only if, we actually take control. As entrepreneurs, we can be working all the time—and I can testify to that because I have been there. Even now, I have to draw my boundaries consciously, revisit some of the Pillars, and say no to some fantastic opportunities.

I applied the five Foundational Pillars myself, and I applied them to the different stages in my life—asking: What are the seven areas, or the big stones? What are the "big rocks," as referred to the late Stephen Covey? For me, this meant asking: *What are the priorities that I constantly need to have in my mind and on my dashboard?*

⁂ ⁂ ⁂

"Surprisingly, I think the biggest challenge for today's young women is that they have so many options. They have so many choices, and I think that can be crippling. I mean, for me, I went to law school because that was the obvious path for a girl with a lot of opinions. And now, I really do think you could be everything. And I do believe you can have it all—as long as you have a great spouse and a really good nanny."
—**Nancy Lublin**, CEO, Do Something. (AOL On Relationships channel, "Nancy Lublin: Too Many Relationships" video. April 6, 2012)

A dashboard is a tool that we use as 24-Hour Women so that we can keep constant perspective as we interact with and apply our day-to-day tasks of systemizing, simplifying, and bundling. This tool allows us to move towards our legacies—and not just live and interact with the seven areas without achieving the outcomes we want. We will discuss the dashboard more in Chapter 7.

You can achieve your legacy, too, as long as you apply the five Foundational Pillars and are able to look at the seven areas in your life so that there's a line towards the legacy you want to leave behind. It's possible!

Taking It Home: Five Simple Ways to Minimize a Caregiver's Interruptions

As working moms, sometimes we envy those who enjoy the flexibility and freedom of working from home. But wait until you hear some of the challenges we have while working from home! Just as you manage interruptions at the office or workplace, there are interruptions that we need to manage when working from home, too. At the top of that list are the interruptions that a caregiver receives. Are you ready to consider working flexibly at home while fulfilling your caregiver role? Here are five tactics that you need to take note of to set yourself up for success. Read on!

1. **Set up boundaries around working at home**. Have a separate space where you work to minimize having to search for office items in the midst of toys (or healthcare products, when you provide elder care). A separate location also serves as an invisible demarcation that you are at work.

2. **Remember that you are working at home, but others around you for whom you are providing care may not realize that.** When they need help, they may still expect that you attend

to them immediately. If you keep responding promptly, however, you may end up constantly being interrupted from your work routine. Be clear about what situations you will provide immediate attention for and which ones will require them to wait. Provide alternatives such as, "Yes, we will fix the cable receiver once I am done with..." or, "Mommy will play with you once...is done. Would you like to complete...first on your own?"

3. **Let the people you are looking after—whether they are children or elderly adults—know your plan for the day, if possible, so that they know you are focusing on work during those periods.** They will also know when you are available for them.

4. **Just as you have an agenda for the day, it also would help to develop a schedule jointly with the kids or elderly adult so that they are also meaningfully and gainfully occupied and engaged.** This builds a sense of routine, which would be most helpful to organizing timely interactions and mutual events.

5. **Be pro-active in looking out for things at home that might need your attention before they happen—just like preparing for any needs an employee or colleague might have in the workplace.**

There you have it: my five steps to minimizing a caregiver's interruptions. (You may also download the checklist and planning chart for this at www.The24HourWoman.com/Resources)

Enjoying the flexibility and freedom of working from home does take some effort and preparation, but it's totally worth it for you to thrive in dealing with the dual role of work and family needs.

What other tips or ideas do you have regarding telecommuting or working from home? Email me at solutions@The24HourWoman.com.

I would love to hear your ideas, and I am sure you will inspire and encourage others.

The 24-Hour Woman Speaks

Ms. Jessica Mastors (US)

Speaker, Story Coach, and

"Lifelong Dream Achiever and Adventurer"

Jessica's unconventional career path began with a simple desire to travel and see the world. She had her first taste of "the huge disparity that exists in the world" when she spent some weeks living with a host family in rural Costa Rica in 2003. The service trip was humbling and inspiring, instilling in her a sense of purpose and also revealing the power that language has to "open the world up."

With the intention of starting a non-governmental organization to address the inequality she'd witnessed, Jessica went on to major in international development studies at McGill University, with a regional focus on South Asia.

At her graduation ceremony, she described seeing a friend wearing a shirt that read: "EDUCATED." The implication—that once you're done with school, there's nothing left to learn—struck Jessica as "totally absurd." She decided to leave the classroom environment and continue learning through firsthand experience. Looking back, this is when Jessica started thinking about the word *educated*, and, as she stated in an interview with me, "looking critically at the stories we grow up with, and the stories we tell ourselves about what's worth doing and learning."

Jessica made a list of all the things she wanted to do in her lifetime, *as though time and money were in infinite supply.* She says this was crucial: "We spend so much time operating within those limits. If we never give ourselves the freedom to imagine that they're not limits, we end up underestimating what we can do with what we've got."

She emphasizes today that dreams require listening to our instincts, but "we have so many people telling us what we *should* dream about, and what we *should* want to do and have in our lives, that we get divorced from our instincts." For this reason, Jessica suspended the logical question of "why" and listened to her gut, trusting that "every experience, no matter how small or seemingly insignificant, teaches you something—if you're looking to learn." It's only in retrospect, she argues, that you "start to see the patterns" that make up your story.

On her list was to journey through India by train. This was one of the countries about which she supposedly was "educated." While there, she spent ten days at a silent meditation retreat, where she realized that "organizations are made of people. A dysfunctional person will build a dysfunctional organization." As she stated in our interview, "I had to figure myself out before I could build anything bigger than me."

This was an important insight and turning point for Jessica, but also a painful one that forced her to surrender old ideas and assumptions. After a period of feeling lost again, she turned to her list—and chose the adventure that would ultimately, as she states, "transform the way I see the world… and what I'm capable of doing in this life."

This transformation happened over a six-month, two-thousand-mile journey on foot over the Appalachian mountain range, from Georgia to Maine. Jessica then began speaking to groups about her hiking experience, always grounding her stories in the fundamental question: "What makes a good education?"

This experience gave rise to a broader discussion with local education leaders in her home state of Rhode Island, one of whom invited her to give a TEDx talk—a dream that Jessica had added to her goal list less than a year before.

In her TEDx talk (titled "Climb with Daring, Fall with Purpose"), Jessica spoke of climbing mountains and the bigger metaphor of achieving something that seems at first to be impossible. In my interview with her, she said, "Whether it's a literal mountain, or it's a psychological mountain, or it's in your career, in your personal life, whatever it is... Anything that's really hard, you get to the top of that first mountain, and that's when you glimpse how many more there are to go. And the only way that you get to the top of a mountain is by tearing your gaze away from the summit, looking down at your feet, and saying, 'Okay, what's the next step? What's the next step? And the next one?'"

Titling the talk "Climb with Daring" came from the Golden Rule of the Appalachian Trail: *hike your own hike.* Jessica saw this as a metaphor for living one's own life; not waiting for someone to tell you how to do it, but deciding that you're willing to "carry your own weight" and work hard for the life that you want. Those who accept this responsibility are "those who get all the benefit...from pushing yourself in that way and from deciding to create your own truth."

The "Fall with Purpose" portion of her title came from a health challenge Jessica endured the following year, after an attack of Guillain-Barré syndrome left her, ironically, unable to walk at all. The doctors insisted it would take at least six months to recover, but because she applied the trail lesson of taking it "one step at a time," she ended up recovering in just three months. Though some called it a miracle, Jessica was adamant that "it was a conscious choice." She said, "I believed that it was possible and focused all my energy around that belief."

Seeing the ability to be present as a connecting thread between her two-thousand-mile hike and her successful recovery, Jessica began taking her meditation practice seriously. She explained that, paradoxically, giving up two hours a day to "do nothing" actually made her *more* productive, by increasing her mental clarity and ability to focus. She said that meditation has enabled her to get things done much more quickly, and might be the best-kept secret of becoming more productive.

If Jessica has a piece of advice for her generation, it's to start consuming experiences, rather than stuff. "This is how you start making discoveries that are meaningful, instead of just entertaining. You start discovering what you like, what you're good at, who you might want to be, what you might want to do, and what this life might mean for you. And meaning, I think, is what we're all seeking." It is up to us, she says, to create the meaning we seek.

But, she cautions, getting other people to see the value of your choices depends on your conviction and your ability to draw connections between what you did and how it has made you, for example, a better leader or a global thinker. "When you don't have the words to describe why that experience was so valuable, people don't get it. You can know, in your heart, all that value, but if you can't communicate it to another person, it gets lost and people will just see it as a gap in your résumé."

For Jessica, this is why *story* is so powerful—it is what connects the dots of your choices, and what makes the arc of your actions meaningful to others. For people and for businesses, she believes that nothing is more powerful than the stories we tell, through both our words and actions.

So her question is essentially this: What's *your* story? What's your big *why*, around which all of your choices are organized?

Jessica has one more piece of advice: when you encounter a "dream poacher" (someone who dismisses your dreams), respond with compassion. Instead of shutting down, ask what happened to make this person see the world that way—and invite him or her to share with you. When you do this, she claims, dream poachers "melt" into the dreamers they really are at heart.

"Everybody is just waiting for an opportunity to have their dreams taken seriously. For that permission to say, 'Yes. You can think about this, you can dream about this, you can act on this, you can do it.' Everybody is just waiting for that affirmation."

And *you* have the power to give it.

Want to watch the full interview? Come on over to www.The24HourWoman.com/blog. Share your comments with me, and ask your questions. I would love to hear from you!

Signpost for Chapter 6

It's time to take action. Yes, you can be a happier and more fulfilled 24-Hour Woman. You've seen the examples and the conversations with Uncommon Women. What have you learned? You are not starting from zero; you already have some of the Pillars in place! Build on them, and see the shift to thriving in your work, business, and life. Consider these questions as you reflect on Chapter 6:

1. What did you learn from the journey of the 24-Hour Women mentioned in this and previous chapters? Share your discoveries with at least five different people. Discuss your learning points and what behaviors you want to model.

2. Watch the TEDx talk, "Climb with Daring, Fall with Purpose." Revisit your purpose and legacy dreams. Share them with your growth friends.

3. What are three things you will start doing right now to move yourself closer towards becoming a happy and fulfilled 24-Hour Woman?

Chapter 7

DOS AND DON'TS

"Don't do what you have been called to do,
do what you are meant to do."
–Paul Martinelli

$\mathcal{W}$omen across the globe, and even I, now and again get things wrong. There are a few strategies, however, which, if you are mindful of, will help you avoid detours and destruction.

Five Don'ts (AVOID These as Much as You Can)

The first "don't do" strategy is *to avoid short-term thinking*. I'm not saying avoid short-term planning, which is very helpful—but rather short-term thinking. This means that you don't want to do something that's a quick fix right now, if it will cost you more down the road.

Remember, we're talking about building towards your legacy—which operates on a longer horizon. Very often, it is that tension between the short-term and the long-term plan that gets people confused or stuck. Invest in the long-term.

For example, if you were running a business and addressing immediate problems with only a "bandage on the wound" solution, that pain/issue will come back to hurt you again because the actual issue will not be resolved. This is your life, and you are in it for the long haul, so think about your decisions in terms of your legacy versus just the short-term. *What can you achieve today to make tomorrow more fruitful?*

The second "don't do" strategy to achieving your legacy is to *avoid becoming overwhelmed.* Let's pause here for a moment. You may think out loud, "Oh my goodness! I have to remember the five Pillars, the seven areas, and then the strategies and then the…? I'm not going to get through this!" *Do not* be overwhelmed—by the processes in this book, or by your own milestones in reaching your legacy. Remember, you have traveled over distance to arrive where you are right now; you're already seeing progress and success! We all start somewhere, so it's perfectly natural that you'd still have distance to travel.

The very fact that you're reading *The 24-Hour Woman* is because you realize that you can proactively do some things to affect the outcome of your life and legacy. I am here to be your guide. I am here to take you through this, step-by-step, so that you don't need to feel overwhelmed. The online community also is here to show you what they have found; you can learn from them, too!

You do not have to learn things the hard way, but you do have to take action. Along those lines, the third "don't do" strategy is to *avoid delaying your life legacy session.* Block out time, and take action. Reserve time to discover what your true passion and legacy are about. Block out time to discover what brings vibrancy and fulfillment to your life. At the end of the day, if you were to block out just fifteen minutes every single day to journal, within thirty days, I bet that you would discover what actions bring you fulfillment and happiness. Why not be the 24-Hour Woman who is full of joy? Fifteen minutes is all you need to start with! What are you waiting for?

The fourth "don't do" strategy is to *avoid doing things randomly.* When you act without intention, you do not know what worked or didn't work. What will help you move forward? You won't know if you are only behaving randomly. Instead, systematically go through this process of discovering yourself as a 24-Hour Woman. This is a tried and proven process. It may take some time, but your life is one that's worth living if it is vibrant and fulfilled. Systematically go through the processes outlined in this book and discover the various fabrics that fit into *your* life. Then, weave the pieces together to form a textured, beautiful tapestry. If you are looking for smaller, day-to-day pieces, look for the role models, templates, and tools that will guide you through. Choose those things that fit your life plan and goals, and not those that are based on someone else's dream.

The fifth "don't do" strategy is to *avoid starting a plan without following through.* Dedication is one of the key characteristics of a 24-Hour Woman, and that's one of the reasons why I would advise you take time to review your plans and whatever you're going through every quarter. Do not leave your planning until the end of the year when people traditionally do their resolutions or visioning. Life is ongoing, so you need to review and adjust your goals regularly. Every quarter, take time to make sure that you are aligned. Further define and refine your legacy as you go, because the clearer you are, the sharper your focus will be.

We've explored the five "don't do" strategies to staying on track with your goals. Another way of looking at this is to flip the strategies and say that there are five things that you really *should get started doing.* They are not difficult; they just take a little bit of time and effort on a daily basis. Consistently work—on a daily basis—tending to the tapestry until it's done. Remember that you have the 24-Hour Woman community available. You have *The 24-Hour Woman* book, online program, and "High Performance Coaching and Mastermind for Women" program to support you every step of the way. All of these resources are made available to you because I believe our lives should be vibrant and fulfilled.

Three Ways to Use Technology (Without Being a Slave to It)

What a delight when we finally did not need to queue up for a pay phone because we had the little gadget called a cell phone or mobile phone in the palm of our hands. What convenience, what freedom!

Mention the words "women" and "technology" together, and it might conjure up images of individuals embarking on a faster pace of life in a 24/7, flatter world, where technology has transformed what used to be time-consuming chores into quick, convenient ones. Most of us would agree that technology has touched virtually every aspect of our world—in our personal sphere (think iPhone), in our workplace (consider virtual collaborative tools), and in our home (all the domestic consumer products and home entertainment systems). Technology has certainly enabled women to take on more roles in the workplace. In roles and industries that were previously predominantly male-dominated or workplace-bound, technology has leveled the playing field, enabling work to be done in different manners altogether.

There is no denying that technology has brought new dimensions—and implications—to both work and non-work areas. Let's take a closer look at three of these spheres.

1. Technology in the Personal Sphere

Mobile phones and laptops often are cited as the tools used most often in the personal sphere. Certainly, the ability for women to have accessibility and be accessible has enabled them to remain connected in their professional and personal roles—even if they are on the go.

With text messages and tweets, we possess more information than ever about what is happening around us, but could technology also be preventing us from building deeper ties? I frequently communicate with my family and friends via text messages throughout the day. However, while there is a place for technology that keeps us connected at a certain level, there are active steps needed on our part to cement relationships on a deeper level. Nothing beats sitting down, having a face-to-face conversation, and spending quality time together. Such "human" moments are crucial and necessary for deep and genuine relationships.

With the iPhone, MP3 players, and handheld games being constant companions, I know of individuals—particularly women—whose only "downtime" or "me" time is the daily commute. Hence, these mobile gadgets, while entertaining and enjoyable, can also distract us from truly enjoying times of solitude and reflection that nourish our souls and well-being. People may be getting a form of ME time in terms of time alone with the gadgets, but it is just entertainment, and not fulfillment.

2. Technology at Home

Women, rather than men, more often than not undertake the caregiving or nurturing roles. In order for women to continue to meet their dual roles in the workplace and home, the innovation of many time-saving appliances we have in our homes today have freed us to better manage these roles. Those appliances have freed us of chores that might have enslaved generations of women before us. They also have leveled the playing field between genders, as the men in the household now can press the button for the washing and drying devices or coffee maker, and in so doing, help out with household chores that might have previously been the women's responsibility.

3. Technology at the Workplace

In my opinion, the greatest innovation in information technology is seen in the workplace. These innovations have impacted women dramatically over the past four decades. The combined force of these innovations have allowed women to play more active, strategic, and value-added roles in their organizations.

Organizations where men and women are equipped with the technology to telecommute or work remotely have seen outcomes where men and women enjoy both dynamic careers and successful family/personal lives. This ability to accommodate both work and non-work needs is very important, particularly for women (and now increasingly also for men as gender roles adapt), as we embark on different life stages.

The freedom to work "whenever" and "wherever" is a cornerstone to enabling and empowering more women in the workplace. Smart organizations have realized the value of leveraging technology that facilitates telecommuting, collaboration, and just-in-time information (through handhelds)—all useful tools to keep women engaged and growing in their careers.

For the many women who have had to leave the workforce because the technology and work culture were not as empowering as they are today, this change might have come too late. **But moving forward, technology in the workplace will continue to level the playing field for more women to contribute strategically to their organizations.**

Technology is also a double-edged sword. While it creates many opportunities and affords us new levels of flexibility and freedom, it also opens a whole Pandora's box of contradicting rules: in a 24/7 world where we are always accessible, what is considered "non-work" time? Participants in our LifeWorkz "StepUp for Women" program have remarked that they receive emails or calls even when they are on leave, or on weekends, simply because they can now be reached remotely. How should they respond? Hence, one of the key skills needed for women today is the ability to negotiate with their bosses and peers as to their "accessibility expectations"—while maintaining the ability to deliver results as needed.

Technology: Enhancing or Robbing Us of Life?

Perhaps ultimately, every woman needs to ask herself if technology is enabling her to enjoy life, or enslaving her to 24/7 connectivity, communications, and "driven-ness." Do we have the freedom to enjoy the simplicity of life and smell the roses along the way? Or are we frantically keeping up with the latest tweet and letting life pass us by?

One mom I know had to keep one eye on the soccer game her son was playing in, and the other on her Blackberry. The result? She found it doubly stressful; she neither enjoyed the game nor accomplished her task. Multi-tasking creates new demands on our lives and adds to our stress, and has in fact proven to be counter-productive.

Yet that same technology can be used to capture wonderful memories and the delightful moments that add to our enjoyment of life—such as photos that can be uploaded for friends and family near and far to access.

Putting It Into Practice

Let's be purposeful in our use of technology, so that it does not become mindless chatter. Here are some tips to keep you grounded amidst the buzz of technology. You will want to address:

- **Technology in the Personal Sphere.** These are tools for your own personal productivity or organization, such as Skype or an online calendar. Specifically identify what technology you need and how you want it to work for you. For a few days, pay attention to how technology is used in your life, and see if it works the way you want it to. Decide if it's really helping to make life better rather than more complex or stressful. Remember, you set the rules of how you will use this technology.

- **Technology in the Home.** My favorite pieces of home technology are the juicer and coffee maker, followed by the oven. Nothing fancy or earth shaking, but these have helped me through numerous mornings. In the morning rush, I get a healthy dose of juices. In the evenings, I can create a fuss-free, grilled salmon for dinner without needing to clean the kitchen extensively—which can become very oily when Chinese wok frying. There are lots of gadgets to choose from. You may indulge or just go for those that you need and know you will use. But remember, sometimes we buy gadgets that we never will use again. The 24-Hour Woman does not have time to waste in this area! Be mindful of your purchases.
- **Technology in the Workspace.** A galore of choices exist here—from cloud-based tools to handhelds, to machinery to make manual work easier. Again, choose what works for you and your team. I work with a distributed team from all over the world. We leverage on various platforms for planning, updates, and connections. Explore and experiment with your team until you find the best technology fit.

One respondent to a LifeWorkz survey relating to women's use of technology said it well: **"Technology can be both a great friend who enables us to lead a satisfying life, or a monster which enslaves us if we do not set limit to its usage."**

So is technology your friend or your foe? The choice is yours to make. Be wise.

Five MUST Dos

1.Define Your Legacy

The first "must do" is to spend time right now, and define your legacy. I realize I have mentioned legacy already, but I'm mentioning it again because it is so important. It may take you a bit of time, and it may not be done in one sitting. It helps to start journaling. Every single day, spend fifteen minutes journaling. What makes you fulfilled and happy? Every time you journal, think about who you would like to be at the end of the day. Ask yourself: *At my eighty-fifth birthday, what would I like people to say about me? What's my career legacy going to be about? What's my relationship legacy going to be about? What's my legacy going to look like in terms of my health? How about my beliefs?* How would you define your legacy?

2.Develop Your Dashboard

Second, create a dashboard that works for you where you can list your legacy—and the priorities, goals, and tactics you are using to achieve that legacy. I love to have everything in one place as a quick reference, so I do not have to scramble all over for things. I have written my legacy on a board that I display near my desk, and I have corresponding tools in place to support achieving that legacy. An example of a tool that could contribute to your dashboard is a calendar that displays every activity in which you and your family are involved—all in one place so that you know if there is an area that you need to scale back a bit in order to make more time for other important things. You may find other tools for creating a dashboard. Find a method that works so you can view your priorities and goals at a glance.

The dashboard exists to help you keep the legacy piece always top of mind. It also helps you to see which five Pillars come into play in the seven different areas of your life. It also highlights the support systems you need to develop. *Who are the people you need to interact with? If you were to bundle networking with another activity, what would it be?* The dashboard helps you keep a picture of your long-term legacy and also your day-to-day actions. It helps you refine what you need to address so that you can make the best use of your day-to-day time and energy.

When I work with women, one of the ways to bring about the quickest change is for them to assess and revise their dashboards. To them, at first it seems like it's just another work plan. But it's not. I don't want you to approach it as just another work plan, but rather a plan for attaining vibrancy in your life. What would put a sparkle into your plan? That plan will become your drive and motivation.

3. Determine Block-out Time.

The next big "must do" is to schedule your "block-out" time. We have discussed the importance of "ME" time. Block-out time may include ME time, or it may simply involve taking a break from your routine to look at your life from a different perspective. It is a tool to create deliberate space for examining your priorities. Block-out time consists of time you set aside either for your health, to learn new things, to renew your mind, or to break the habit of thinking about work. This is essential not just for journaling, as you need to break your routine in order to focus on your life strategy, but also for your own renewal.

While you develop and gain clarity on your legacy, and work to apply the five Pillars and seven areas, you also need to replenish and nourish yourself, especially if you have been neglected. You should also start thinking about hobbies; if you love to read, when was the last time you picked up something to read that was not work related? Begin to diversify a bit more, because doing so might also give you a sense of feeling really alive and happy. Decide whether you want your block-out time to include plays or renewal—or both. When you block out time just to nourish yourself, you begin to learn more about yourself, so it adds to your discovery process.

4. Determine Who Are Your "Growth" Friends

If you have not identified your growth friends, do it now, because you will lean on them as you make your transition towards your legacy. I learned the term *growth friends* from my mentor, Brendon Burchard. We will discuss them more in Chapter 8, but for now, understand that these are the people you hang out with who will grow with you and have your back. Growth friends are a critical support in times of transition or when times get tough. They'll be the ones who give you a call every evening to say, "Hey, have you done your journaling? Tell me about your day."

If you're not somebody who loves to journal, have a girlfriend who is willing to invest in you, because she will give you a call and spend time talking to you for fifteen minutes—just asking you questions. Then, you'll be able to reflect back on that conversation and write down or act on what was key for you. If you're always left to your own devices, writing may be a very painful process; but if you have a conversation with someone about the things you are trying to sort out, the process is much easier. If someone can tell you, "You know, you just sounded different when you talked about that. You sounded so excited about it," then you can take note, because that might be an area that really brings you vibrancy and fulfillment. Ask yourself: *How does that fit into the seven areas of my life? How can I amplify it through appreciation, awareness, acceptance, accountability, and action?* Those are the building blocks that you need to have in place.

5.Discover Your Beliefs

One of the areas where we perhaps do not spend sufficient time is around our beliefs. If we believe that we must live vibrant and joyful lives, that belief becomes our motivation and drive for making it happen. If you don't feel that "I should do this" or "I deserve it," then you'll be discounting your efforts and unlikely to arrive passionately at your goal. **The most important question to ask and talk about is:** *what do you believe?* **Because the outcome then becomes your theme song.** (Can you imagine what emotions that song can create when it plays in your head?) This question creates the mindset that gets you to think big and gets you to think of what is possible. It is the gateway for you to get into that space of being authentically yourself.

If I could suggest one thing that you should start considering right now, it would be to remove any ideas, teachings, or comments you have heard growing up that said, "Well, this is life. You've just got to live it as is." If you believe that you should have a life that's vibrant and joyful, then invest in that belief. When you invest, you gain a sense of control, and also a sense of congruence, because deep down within you want to experience a fulfilled, vibrant, and joyful life.

When your dreams and your actions are aligned, it is so much easier to flow. When you need to make that shift or change and say no to people, you will thrive in that change, because you will be consciously designing an outcome that you're looking forward to. So let yourself know that you can have a life that's vibrant and fulfilled. Give yourself permission, and tell others, "My goal is to leave a legacy that is (this, this, and this), and I want to live a life that's vibrant and joyful despite all of the craziness and madness that's going on around us." For all you know, you may find supporters among those people.

What I'm sharing with you is not rocket science. You probably have heard it a thousand times. The most prominent adversities people face are made of precisely the same old things that are holding us back: *our fears*. We ask: "What if I were to change? What does that mean? If I were to change, what if I fail? If I were to change, that means I've got to spend time doing new stuff; how do I do that?" It's scary! That's why we fall back on our old ways.

But if you feel that you should have a vibrant and joyful life, then you should have that life. Fears should not stand in your way.

The fear is never real, because the changes it brings help us get to a better place—even if it's uncomfortable at first. For example, Esther needed something drastic to happen, like her child's response to her caregiver, to cause her to think about her legacy and say, "If one of the characteristics of my legacy is that I'm a great mom—a mom whom her child loves and has a close relationship with—then I need to be doing something differently." When you know why you are changing, there will be no fear of that change or *whether people like you*—or thoughts of, "What happens if I fail?" Because even if you fail, you will have tried, and your relationship should certainly be better as a result. For Esther, that was it; she said, "If I don't make the effort, I will never know. But if I make the effort, I know it will be better."

Fear is certainly one of the things holding us back. What are some of the things we can do to change it? I can tell you, and I can share with you, but you are the one who needs to have the awareness, acceptance, and accountability—and take the action.

The second adversity besides fear that we know gets in the way is that *we are creatures of habit*. Sometimes we get into a rhythm with our own habits and need to stop ourselves to say, "Hey, as part of taking accountability and action, I need to forget some of those practices and habits and get new ones." Part of the process could involve taking a thirty day challenge to build a new habit or break a habit. Again, doing so would take time, but it's time worth investing in—as long as you know that you want to become a 24-Hour Woman.

You want to be fulfilled and happy at the end of the day, and at the same time, look behind you and see your legacy being developed through your habits.

The third adversity we face is that we feel that we're on this journey alone. That image invokes fear. But, if you look around—if you begin to build your growth friends right now; if you get involved in our online community, training program, or coaching program for women leaders—you will find a lot more support out there globally, and many of these women have already made transitions. Many of them might be ready to transition with you. Who would be better company for you than another woman going through similar changes? These people have walked the path you will be walking and are going on a journey together with you.

I'm always available and interacting in the online community to offer support, to answer questions, to serve as a coach, and also to train members on some of the latest "know-hows" in order to work through the five Pillars and different areas of life. You might not need all of them now, but you will in other life stages as you journey on.

Often, people give advice and comments. They are probably doing so out of good intention, but *they are not you*. You need to take their good intentions and advice and consider the outcome on your life. Consider the impact of following their suggestions on your legacy, because some of what they say may actually derail you. Which is, once again, why it's important for you to be building growth friends, because they will know what you're really about—and not about. Hopefully, they have the same belief and view that you should have a vibrant and joyful life; but again, they are not you. Take their comments and advice, and you can take my comments and advice; but at the end of the day, I would love to give you the wheel and let you steer your own journey.

Great Starting Point

There are a couple of areas that I think we need to think through again so that we start moving in the right direction. If you are not living a vibrant and joyful life, ask yourself *why you are investing in things that are not bringing you in that direction.* The answer might cue you in to one of the seven areas of life—beliefs—and whether you are in alignment with yours. **Because what you believe, you manifest. It's not just what our parents taught us or what the school system teaches or what the media is saying that gets us where we need to go; it's what *we* believe, and what we do with those beliefs, that matters most.**

We really need to think through and ask ourselves, "Who am I? Who do I want to be?" For me, my beliefs strongly center around who I believe my God says I am. Fundamentally, I know that I am called for success, and I'm called to be a blessing, and I'm called not to do this on my own. I'm reassured that He will provide all of the resources I will need. That's my belief. Similarly, there are some fundamentals that you've got to ask yourself in order to make measurable and consistent progress: *What do you believe in? Who do you believe you are?* The answers are fundamental.

When things get challenging, if you have a belief system in place, you will then dig deep within yourself to say, *it will pass, and my reality will come to pass.* It's not easy, particularly when you do not feel that you have a very supportive environment. I use myself as an example; my parents were both teachers. When I graduated, the first job they wanted me to take, of course, was a teaching position. To satisfy them, I spent a year teaching, and I absolutely loved it; but I realized it was not my key passion.

I took on a corporate role. My parents were very apprehensive because their belief was that a corporate job would not be secure; a teaching job, which was a state job, a public sector job, was secure. They came from a post-war context wherein their mentality was largely about security. That was and is their reality.

In situations like this, where someone else who may influence you holds a different reality, you need to be able to say, "That's this person's reality, and that's why she has her belief." Then, look at the situation and ask, "What is my context right now?" and, "This is my reality." That's where you define what you believe you can achieve.

When I left my corporate job and started my own business, even though I loved what I did after transitioning, the cycle of questioning came back all over again. Even up to this day, my parents ask me, "When are you going to get a real job?" They don't believe that running a business is a real job—particularly when a lot of my transactions or encounters with clients create friendships as I teach and train them. Plus, I meet all of them through life events. They can't believe there is a job that would pay someone to do all of that.

This is my reality, and my belief is that I can touch lives and make a difference by enjoying what I do *and* making a difference in other people's lives. I do this by showing people that it can be done and by helping people get it done—in the corporate arena, in their personal lives, and in their own businesses if they are entrepreneurs.

As I said, the biggest thing you have working for you is your own belief system. Even though beliefs are among the most constant factors you have to guide you, there will be changes over time to your beliefs from the past and even present. You can look at them, and if they are limiting your potential, you can ask yourself, "Am I worth more?" If you do think that you're worth more, that's an indicator that it no longer needs to be your belief.

The people we see who make the greatest transitions or leaps are those who deal with beliefs first—and define their legacies based on their beliefs. They do not look at creating and optimizing the five Pillars and the seven areas of their lives just as a planning exercise. They really think through what it means to be a 24-Hour Woman, and they hold themselves accountable to their beliefs and plan. They take action.

If a woman "sort of" knows where she wants to go but does not have a plan, defining her beliefs is a great place to start. The most challenging part then becomes developing clarity on where she wants to go.

Once you have defined your beliefs, you can ask, "These are the big pieces. Is this stage in life aligned to where I want to be going?" Then, ask: "What are the day-to-day behaviors that would be supportive to me? What are some of the habits? What are some of the things I need to make sure to schedule? Who can I call upon? How can I work things through?"

Then ask: "What can I simplify? How can I systemize? Who are the people I will reach out to in order to build my support system in my personal and professional life?" These are the tools and steps or templates that we have in this book and in our training programs to help you define the greater details of who you are. In the book, there's only so much we can cover; likewise, there are some elements in the online program that we cannot produce in a book—purely because of the conversations and team element. The conversations that we have add richness to the online program and our live events. So I recommend that you check out both the book and the online resources to maximize your discovery process.

If you already have a sense of clarity, the online templates will walk you through the process. And of course, I'm there for anyone who wants a little more one-on-one time. There's always an avenue for conversation. The beautiful thing is that you can start where you're comfortable. *Just start.*

Sometimes in life, we have a few naysayers who are not actually supportive of our journeys. They are not growth friends. What if one such person is your husband or someone who is very close to you? That's very often the first person who you need to work with when you get into this process. I would put it to them very gently and say, "Would you like a vibrant and joyful version of me every day, or somebody who is grouchy all the time?" We also have to be mindful that sometimes others do want someone who is vibrant and joyful, but they are afraid. Just like you are afraid to make those changes, they are afraid that if you change, you might find that they are not who you would like to be around. Therefore, they'd rather you *not* change.

You need to reassure others to be on the journey with you—particularly if it's your spouse or a close family member. You can't change a spouse or another person; you instead need to help the person understand why you need this change. Explain your belief about who you are and your belief about what value this change will bring to the relationship. Share how the relationship can grow through the change. It is about *influencing*. You have to remain congruent to convince this person to stay on the journey with you.

When I decided to start my own business, it was because I wanted more time with my children. My husband was very apprehensive. It took us three years to think about it, pray about it, and just make it settle before we made a decision.

As you make changes, there will be some things that will take time to work through and unfold. If you are congruent and consistent and don't give up, even though it's tough, you will work through those areas a little bit at a time.

Progress is not about just working at it every single day, but always keeping the big picture in mind. Do not forget the big picture amidst being so busy with day-to-day actions. Sharing the big picture with your partner or other close loved one is also important in helping that person stay motivated to support you. How can you bring this person on your journey while managing this person's fears and anxieties? You are going to live a more vibrant and joyful life, but what about him or her? That's something you need to take into consideration, so you are not only growing individually—but in your relationship.

☀ ☀ ☀

"One, I always chose to work with the smartest and most interesting people I could find. And two, I always did something I was a little not ready to do. And I remember in each case thinking, 'wow, what have I really got myself into?' But I've found that if you push through that feeling of being scared, that feeling of taking a risk, really amazing things happen."
—**Marisa Mayer**, CEO, Yahoo, (Taylor, Felicia. CNN, "Google's Marissa Mayer: Passion Is a Gender-Neutralizing Force." April 5, 2012)

☀ ☀ ☀

Taking It Home: Great Technology for Caregivers

As a working mom, daughter, and grand-daughter, I am always on the lookout for systems or technology that will make fulfilling my caregiver roles more efficient and effective. As our population ages, more of us—single or married—will take on caregiver roles. What are my choices regarding technology as a caregiver?

1. **With an Elderly Adult.** For many I work with, their main concern is safety. They want to ensure that their parents take any required medication when needed. This is particularly the concern for those who live in different cities from their parents. Here are some ideas:
   - Some rely on a mobile phone for alerts and to call their parents, which can get extremely costly and become impractical. Making use of a life event company such as LifeCare (see www.LifeCare.

com) can be helpful, so that a parent's well-being is always monitored for medical appointments or medication timing.

- Phones and remotes with larger keypads or headphones are useful so the user experience is enhanced, instead of making an older adult struggle with mis-keying on the phone or accidentally blasting the volume to enjoy their favorite sitcoms.

2. **With Children**. When you are a mother, I suggest the following:
- Implement scheduling devices so that everyone is in sync with what's happening for the day or week. I still practice a dual system by having a huge calendar on my fridge for reference, especially by grandparents or other caregivers—along with my electronic calendar in the cloud.
- Dropbox is great, too, for mothers to keep documents or pictures, etc., that she wants to share with the rest of the family. It also can house forms that need to be completed and sent back to school.
- Mobile phones are perfect to capture the moments in pictures, video, or audio and share them with the rest of the family.

What other tips or ideas do you have regarding the role of being a caregiver either to young children or elderly adults? Email me at solutions@The24HourWoman.com. I would love to hear your ideas, and I am sure you will inspire and encourage others.

The 24-Hour Woman Speaks
Ms. Emi Takemura (Japan)
Cofounder and Asia Head, Peatix.com

Emi Takemura, cofounder and Asia head of Peatix.com, is another example of a strong woman who had the drive and determination to use the Five Pillars of a 24-Hour Woman to change her unsatisfying situation and create the life she always had imagined. Emi started working in a management consulting firm right after college and eventually switched into the corporate world where she worked as senior manager for Amazon Japan and then marketing director for Disney Japan. Emi appreciated her corporate life and enjoyed the projects that she was able to contribute to.

Because of the culture in Japan, Emi worked hard to readjust and realign her principles to fit into the different corporate cultures. She said:

> *I had to really readjust and realign myself to fit with the Amazon culture, and once you know and fit the culture, it's all about building a rapport and delivering your goal with a team. So it's really about finding how you fit with a new corporate culture and what's the best way to contribute within the new culture, especially when you are starting at the beginning. You really have to prove yourself, that you're a value to the company. So how do you translate the value you created with a previous employer and find your own niche with the new company and new culture? I think that's really the key.*

Emi knew her strengths and used them to her benefit. She took time to build her credibility and then reached out to build a rapport with the other people who she needed support from. Emi used her strengths to navigate her way to a C-level position. She said, "I always like to play to my strengths. So, for example, being a consultant, my analytical skills and strategy-building skills were probably stronger than some of the peers."

Emi appreciated the projects that she was able to be a part of and the skills she learned while working her jobs. But one day, she realized that the life she had built didn't really coincide with having a family. She ultimately decided that this wasn't the career that she wanted. She was aware of the skills she possessed, and knew that they would allow her some flexibility in terms of a career change.

She accepted that this change was going to be a challenge. Uprooting her family to make it happen would be even harder; but it would be a worthwhile move. She said:

Coming to Singapore was a relatively easy decision, because we really felt the market was ready for our type of service. I came here last summer for a few weeks to just evaluate the market, and I felt that the people really could use our type of service; and there's limited competition. So it was an easy decision for just me to come. Bringing the family over was a bigger decision, obviously. And that took quite some time for us to really decide whether it was a good move. But fortunately, we had enough friends in Singapore who informed us about the education and environment here. It is a great, family-friendly country. And at the end of the day, it was a good decision.

Emi took accountability for her life and knew that her dream job wouldn't happen on its own; she needed to be the force pushing this idea. She said: "For me, having flexibility is very important. By being your own boss, you do create flexibility. So that's definitely a big benefit of having your own company. But at the same time, building a team is also quite rewarding."

After years of trying to get all the puzzle pieces in place, Emi finally made the move, quit her job, and co-founded Peatix.com, an event planning company leveraging on technology.

I've always focused on social values, so the reason I wanted to start a consulting firm was I wanted to do something of a greater good. We wanted to really contribute to the creative world and people who have a great passion and want to communicate that passion through events. We wanted to support the people through a platform. So we always start with a kind of social mission and value. We always felt that running events was a necessary vehicle for anybody who likes to realize their passion, whether they're artists, or musicians, or corporate, or people running workshops. So we felt that it had wide enough appeal in the marketplace and there wasn't, at that point in Japan, a very convenient, affordable tool available in the marketplace. So we filled the gap between the needs—and the service and tools.

When asked how she manages such a successful career on top of family life, Emi admitted that scheduling was not always her strong suit. She sought out the use of technology to help her plan her schedules, because her business schedule was always overlapping with her kids' schedule. She said it was a learning process, but technology really helped to manage those overlaps.

When asked to share a little about what kind of legacy she'd like to leave behind, Emi said she'd like to be known, on the business front, for creating great organizers. On a more personal level she said:

I'd like to be known as somebody who helped, who's a role model for other women who like to be their own entrepreneurs. And I feel very fortunate that with all the circumstances, I can have children and have a very fulfilling career. But for some reason, many people think having your own company and managing children, managing those two goals, is very difficult, impossible.

*So I like to be one of the role models that it can be done, and it's
actually very fulfilling.*

Even though Emi was at the top of her field, in a society that wasn't
very well adjusted to women in senior positions in organizations, Emi
realized it wasn't fulfilling her. She had the ability to fix her situation,
and she used the Five Pillars of a 24-Hour Woman to create a *life most
excellent* for herself.

Do you find yourself in a similar situation? How will you use Emi's
story as motivation to create the life you desire?

Want to watch her full interview? Come on over to www.
The24HourWoman.com/blog. Share with me your comments, and ask
your questions. I would love to hear from you!

Signpost for Chapter 7

You've guessed it. It's time to journal. Now, consider these
questions as you reflect on Chapter 7:

1. Of the five Don'ts, which will most likely happen for you? What
   can you do to set yourself up for success instead?
2. Of the five Dos, which would be your low hanging fruit? Which
   would be the toughest for you to handle alone? Well then, don't!
   Get your growth friends on the task with you.
3. Is technology your friend or foe? How can you leverage on
   technology in a massive, 24/7 world?

Chapter 8

BIG MINDSET STUFF

"Taking the first step starts the momentum."
–Cheryl Liew-Chng

*I*n one of my recent interviews, I was asked, "What do you think is the universal first step that keeps people inspired—if there indeed is one that helps them begin their adventure towards more vibrant, joyful, and fulfilled lives?"

One secret to keeping oneself inspired, as I observe in the many women who I work with, is to *always have a physical anchor or cue to remind yourself why you are picking that first step*. It's a reminder as to what you want to achieve, how you want to feel, and what is most important. Finding the physical anchor for this helps you to *keep at it*. It may be a picture or an object or a quote that summarizes the essence of your why. For me, it is a picture of my family.

For many people, their goal may be to attain a certain level of authority within an organization. But to remain inspired through the process, you will need to ask yourself: *Why do I want to be there in the first place? What does it bring me that inspires me?* For you to stay motivated, the first step is not just to "get my million dollars," but rather to answer, "Why do I want a million dollars? What would it mean in my life?"

It's about asking: *Will it mean I can free up time or invest in a better education? Or can I invest in more time spent with my children?* With these questions at the forefront, it becomes easier for you to take the first step—and remain inspired through every step—to gain momentum. You always have to know *why you want to do that specific thing or reach that specific goal.*

I hope that beyond any tangible reminder, your legacy is your motivation as you develop your work plan or blueprint. It's usually the non-tangible that motivates us for the longer term, because it drives deep into our emotions. It works on the simple fact that we want to be happy, we want to be respected, and we want to be fulfilled. Legacy is an intangible. It's the opposite of instant gratification. But if we keep it in our sights, it remains a motivating reason for everything we do.

We *can* meet both our work and life needs at different life stages. Picking the first step changes the scenery. It means looking at what excites you and motivates you at this time in your life. It involves redefining what motivates you to take that first step, and the next, and the next. It's sort of like building a bridge as you cross it.

When you take the first step, you realize that you come from a position of strength, that you can do it, that it becomes a part of your necessary mindset. Your goals ARE achievable once you shift gears from just thinking and planning—into direct action.

Maneuvering the Road Blocks

Our Fears

As we've discussed, a primary roadblock holding you back from taking your first step will be fear. You must face your own fears about change—because you don't know what the outcome will be—and you must face your fears about how the process will unfold and what the sacrifices will be along the way.

Ask yourself: are your fears about how *reaching for your goals may change your relationships with loved ones and people around you?* Those fears sometimes amplify with people closest to you—who, with all good intentions, give their best advice. But often, that advice just amplifies some of *their* fears—and not your reality.

Building your core beliefs such that they are strong, as we've discussed, gives you a head start. What do you value most? The answer to that question will become your "why" and keep you moving toward building your intangible, but most valuable, legacy. Going back to your "why" is what gives you the motivation to deal with the fears. It also gives you the motivation to build new habits.

I realize I'm repeating myself with some of these points, but that's because they are so crucial to our development. Sometimes we need to hear a concept a few times, or see it in a few different frames, before it truly sinks into action.

Understanding how beliefs interplay with your legacy is a key concept that is crucial to becoming a 24-Hour Woman.

It's never easy to shift out of old beliefs or patterns. For example, one of our clients needed to become more visible in order to start her own business. Her thoughts on that reality were, "I'm not someone who wants to be on social media. I don't want my personal life to be told to the world." We began to tell her that if she was going to be in the new economy and showcase her growing business, then she had to put herself out there. How much she would choose to put out there, however, would be up to her to decide.

The question and motivation should not be what she's comfortable with—but rather, what she wants to leave as her legacy. How far she challenges her comfort level and routine all depends on how big she wants her ambition and her dreams to be.

She began to build a new habit, based on a new idea: "I'll craft my Facebook posts, my LinkedIn posts, and my YouTube videos to talk about new things. I can also talk about myself personally—to the degree that I want to be vulnerable." She began to create a new habit of building her online presence—and it worked.

Our Habits

Habits take time to develop. They take consistent, directed efforts. When it comes to your mindset, strongly consider what habits you would need to get started on to create an attitude of success—and to stay the course to hit your ultimate goals. The book, *The Power of Habits*, by Charles Duhigg, is a great resource.

The beauty is in the process, as we grow into a 24-Hour Woman. There is a growing community at www.The24HourWoman.com/blog where you can both contribute and receive support to resolve current challenges. I encourage you to join! My team is also available to help you build new habits—whether they have to do with fears, productivity, or other potential roadblocks. In that support, we're able to move closer to our goals and legacy.

Five Ways to Build Better Friendships and Develop "Growth" Friends

In my interaction with women who found success and thriving in their work/business and life, a common element is their reference to a strong group of women pals who believed in them, journeyed with them, nudged them along, and grew with them. In my interviews with experts who work with women leaders, when I ask them what is one key resource that women need to have, many will say a *support network*.

I learned from my mentor to find and nurture relationships with "growth" friends. These are like-minded individuals who are committed to living vibrant and joyous lives. They are on a similar journey just like you—committed to thriving and growing as a 24-Hour Woman.

I have been blessed over time to have a group of friends who "grew up" together. **Here are my tips for building friendships and nurturing growth friends:** (Be warned, it takes time, understanding, effort, and lots of love and respect for one another to build these relationships.)

1. **Always speak and act out of love for the other person.**
2. **Stand in the gap and listen, because sometimes that's all that is needed. If asked, then give your input.**
3. **Encourage and challenge one another to be your highest selves.**
4. **Be willing to stand by and support one another's dream and efforts.**
5. **Schedule time for one another to connect in a fun manner—and not just for serious discussion.**

Anyone come to mind? I am so grateful that over time, I have found a couple of gals who have fit the criteria of "growth friends." Take time now to consider who might be your growth friends.

Putting It Into Practice

Let's identify your possible growth friends. List the friends who you have known over time and who know you and your aspirations. *You can trust them.* As you look at their lives, you notice a sense of excitement, movement, and growth. Yet, you also sense that they are anchored. They should be the small team of close advisors and confidants who will challenge you and have your back.

How should you nurture these relationships and shortlist your growth friend possibilities?

- **Set aside regular time to spend with one another or as a group.** This can be as simple as sharing a half hour over a cup of coffee or setting aside time to go on breaks together. Talk about your aspirations and ambitions.
- **Identify common needs.** Are there training or development sessions that you can attend together? What areas of growth can you seek together?
- **Engage in active support for one another.** Keep a look-out for resources and people in your network who will add value to your growth friends in their aspirations. Encourage and challenge your growth friends, and ask for the same to be done for you.

When these individuals you have shortlisted reciprocate, nurture the relationships further and be explicit in showing your appreciation for them. Continue developing the relationship as you cultivate longer-term growth friends.

Does a list of growth friends come naturally to you? Great! Continue to nurture these precious friendships. If not, start looking out for them so you can cultivate suitable relationships.

Our Patience (or Persistence)

Another factor that gets in our way of digging into that first step is our ability to estimate and design our desired growth. How much do we want to grow, and how fast do we want to grow? We have seen people who have made dramatic changes because every single day they did something about it. They began to move forward in every way. They looked at ways to simplify. They also looked at ways they could systemize. They looked at ways they could embrace flexibility creatively. In everything they did, they looked for ways they could leverage and ask for help—building their support, even before they needed it.

Once you take creative action, success is dictated by your desire to move towards your legacy, and then your ability to increase momentum. You need to see possibility and move forward with optimism. My definition of legacy may be different from yours, but that's the beauty of it; we're all on our own journey. We have different things that work for us, but we can share and learn from each other.

Even once you know your beliefs, establish your growth friends, and build new habits, there still may be stress along the way as you add in a new goal or habit; but certainly in doing so you will find a more fulfilling and happy life. You will create a journey that inspires you and a legacy towards which you will want to take that first step.

The Naysayers

There are many reasons somebody would be a naysayer. One could be that they wish you would take the safe path. Another inspiration for naysayers could be financial concerns. As you branch into new areas and projects, others may not understand. Sometimes there are expenses involved, and that brings out money worries. So how do you address those naysayers in a way that you do not easily get distracted or tossed into battle? What can you do to put them to the side and still keep your focus?

With the exception of a spouse or some of your closest friends or family members, you can deal with naysayers in a couple of ways. *The first is stay away from them.* There are many times random people will give you their two cents worth even if you do not ask for it. It's up to you to decide if you really need that advice, and then deal with the aftermath of the input—or you can just nip it in the bud and instead gravitate toward people who are supportive of you. If you gravitate toward people who might be on the same journey as you, you'll get the nourishment and care to grow toward your goals.

Remember to avoid conflict; do not go toe-to-toe with the naysayers. You need to conserve your energy to really, really focus and make shifts—cultivating new habits and making new connections.

Here's another fear to tackle head on: when you make those changes, you need to make new friends and connections, and you may fear that you will lose the old. My recommendation for you is, if your old circle of friends is not going to support you, then why do you want to have them in your life? You don't have to deal with them rudely or say they're "talking nonsense"; that would just give all the negativity back to them. Instead, just nicely laugh off their naysaying remarks, and steer clear of them.

This is easy if the person making the remarks is just a teammate, an associate, or even a distant friend; but if that person is one of your closest friends or a family member, then it may be worth finding ways to bring that person in and enlist him or her. Show this person why this legacy means so much to you. It might not win him into your camp overnight, but it might over time. Take myself and my sister as an example. We both became entrepreneurs, and up to this day, as I mentioned, our parents still ask us occasionally, sometimes jokingly, "When are you girls going back to find a real job?"

When it comes to those who are dear to you, it will be very painful if your intention is to cut them off. It will probably be easier on both parties if you can just bring them on your journey. When they see your enthusiasm, when they see how thrilled you are in the shift, in the ability to be more fulfilled, in the ability to smile and express joy, they likely will come around eventually.

Don't forget that they are also fearful, not just for you, but fearful also for what would become of them if you were to change, as we discussed. What does the change mean to them? That might be the reason why they are knowingly unsupportive—or even sabotaging you—instead of supporting you.

Another obstacle we may encounter is that many people may come and talk to us from their best intentions and vast experience; but you must always remember that this is about *you and your legacy*, not somebody else's experience or legacy. These are not somebody else's values; they are your values. So you need to decide that this naysayer is unimportant and keep him or her at arm's length, if that is the case. If it's too painful to surgically remove him or her, ask yourself what you can do to enlighten, influence, and bring this person over to your side.

If talking doesn't work, actions often will. Ask yourself: what can I do in terms of tenacity to show that I mean business? If you can't change someone else's opinion, you will have to decide when to simply continue in your course of action regardless of how that person feels. You deserve to feel vibrant, joyful, and alive, and that will come by staying your course.

How Do You Think You Stay on Track with Your Plan?

I think having points where you claim your successes and celebrate your joys throughout your plan is very helpful. Is it possible to look at your plan and benchmark places where you have hit goals? If yes, create a reward that is meaningful, because benchmarking the *wins* in your hard work is vital—so you don't forget the joy along the way.

In fact, success is not just about achieving goals, but achieving what the goal brings you. If you were able to successfully negotiate flexibility at work, then celebrate it! Enjoy the very flexibility you gained, and take your child or parents out. By using the flexibility to have tea and do something together with someone you love, you solidify the value of your hard work on every level.

Yes, we have an action plan, and as we move through a course of action, we will reach certain milestones. Celebrate them. The celebration is a symbol, not just of your effort, but also of what the experience brought you from a value and legacy point of view.

For example, Jane was exploring whether or not to do a corporate crossover. What she did was a lot of research and online discovery, and she finally built her own company. She got over her roadblock and finally linked it to social media, and she was thrilled when she had her first fifty Facebook likes. She sent us an email and said, "Hey, I'm up to fifty; I'm going for one hundred!"

She also said, *"Before I head out there to build more fans, I'm going out for a cup of coffee with the friend who helped me set up all of my pages."* So for Jane, it was a celebration. It was part of her legacy, at a life stage when she was exploring starting her own business. Ultimately, that milestone gave her the confidence to say, "At this age, I can still learn, and the technology is not going to get me down. Even though I'm in my mid-fifties, starting my next career is a real possibility."

How about this for a celebration: a cup of coffee? Achieving that small goal gave Jane the confidence and self-respect, so she celebrated it with a friend in an inexpensive but tangible way. That type of celebration also builds camaraderie that you can lean on when you're feeling surrounded by haters or wracked with the obvious roadblocks that come up in every woman's life.

Remember what we covered in Chapter 6—that we have to create or discover ways to simplify? Recall: you bundle activities, you systemize, and you look at how often you repeat things. Doing so allows you to do more than one thing—and more than one thing meaningfully, so that it's not just about being efficient. It's also about how effective your actions are.

You grab a coffee, so there's your downtime. You read your book, and that's also your learning time. It's not just about efficiency when you're a 24-Hour Woman. If you're a 24-Hour Woman who wants to be fulfilled, vibrant, and happy, then you've got to look at what you're busy with. You need to be sure you're being efficient and effective, and moving towards your legacy. Your LEGACY is the center, always.

During every single day, remind yourself why you're doing this, and get in the habit of setting boundaries. This creates clear time for you to focus and be productive in doing whatever you do. You are also setting aside clear times when you can build relationships.

Some people do very well when they mix everything together—work, life, and play—all into one, big, muddled ball. But some of us work best when work is separated. You need to know yourself and how you can set boundaries around your own rhythm. Whatever your style, I advocate setting boundaries, because it's also your way of setting expectations with people around you and creating a framework for how they can communicate and interact with you.

Always have a habit of showing appreciation for others and yourself. Often, we forget ourselves. We thank everybody, and then when it comes to ourselves, we say, "No, this is expected of me. I don't deserve gratitude." Thank yourself, because it is something that nourishes you and builds your resilience. When we talk about appreciation, it's not just for others. Appreciate yourself, too. Once in a while, giving yourself a high five won't kill you! Once in a while, telling yourself, "I did an awesome job," won't make you over confident!

≈⊱ ≈⊱ ≈⊱

"She taught me to not to be afraid of failing, which so often holds young women back. She always used to say to me, 'failure is not the opposite of success, it's a stepping stone.' I say the same to my daughters."
—**Arianna Huffington** had this advice for younger women from her mom (BuzzFeed, "Arianna Huffington: It's Time For Women To 'Help Redefine Success.'" February 7, 2013)

≋ ≋ ≋

What other tips or ideas do you have regarding returning to the workplace? I would love to hear your ideas, and I am sure you will inspire and encourage others.

Taking It Home: Help! Which Childcare Is Best for My Child?

Many women who are active in their careers may still choose to place their children in childcare, even if they have the option to work from home. What's best for one household might differ from what's best for another—and needs can change over time. Some of my colleagues' children were in childcare centers before their formal school years; when their children were sick, however, they would telecommute and stay with their children.

The initial process of short listing the best childcare center for your child is one that most parents find challenging to grapple with. In this section, I will share some of the collective wisdom of moms that I had conversations with around their choices or considerations of such a center.

1. **Assess if you want the childcare center to be located near your workplace or near your home.** Take into consideration if you are the main person who will be bringing your child to and fro, or if you might be sharing the responsibility with someone else—particularly in regards to the child's pick-up, if the time you get off work is uncertain.

2. **Examine the physical environment.** Is the center in a built-up area? Does it offer air-conditioning or open ventilation? How polluted is the environment? Would you want your child to be in an enclosed, air-conditioned room; somewhere with cross-wind ventilation and an indoor play area; or a place with a large garden of open space for activities? What is the physical setup of the center, in terms of classes? For example, does it have an open concept (there is a center in Japan that experimented with an open concept and found that the children were more focused as they had to hone in their hearing to the voices of their teachers)? Or does it have designated classrooms?

3. **Learn about the center**. Ask yourself: *What do I expect my child to learn and value in his/her growing up years? Does the philosophy of the center resonate with me and what I want for my child?* Consider the size of the center's intake per class, if its operating hours would meet your needs, and of course, whether the fee structure and mode of payment work for you.

4. **Consider the curriculum and teaching faculty.** It was important for me to consider both my childcare center's approach to its curriculum and its teaching faculty. It's not just important to feel comfortable with the teachers' professional

development, but their attitudes and ability to engage with your child, too. Do they take time with the child and work with the child firmly without breaking his or her spirit?

5. **Look Into Legal Matters.** Make sure that the center has the required licensing and meets the other regulatory requirements— for example, health related, environmentally related, etc.

All moms will have their own sets of criteria; feel free to add yours to this list. The one final step is to visit the centers you are considering and gain a feel of them yourself. Would your child be happy in that environment? Can you see your child playing, having friends, and enjoying his/her learning and growing up years?

What other tips or ideas do you have in considering a childcare center? What have you learned from your past experience in the selection process? Email me at solutions@The24HourWoman.com. I would love to hear your ideas, and I am sure you will inspire and encourage others.

The 24-Hour Woman Speaks
Ms. Natalie Brown (United Kingdom)
Founder, TimeWithNatalie.com

Natalie Brown is, by nature, someone who has always wished to help people. Natalie is the host of "Time with Natalie," a show that highlights women demonstrating how they can put the various stage of their lives together and live their dreams. Natalie didn't always have this career, however. But she used the five Foundational Pillars of the 24-Hour Woman to help achieve her life's successes.

Natalie started her career in finance. She stayed there for almost ten years before eventually realizing that it was not her passion. Natalie wanted more out of her life and knew that a finance career wasn't going to cut it. She was stuck though, relying on the great pay and convenience of a steady job, which kept her from finding her true passion.

Natalie had a nervous breakdown shortly after her revelation, and it knocked her off her feet. She described the situation in a recent interview:

My breakdown mainly consisted of depression coupled with anxiety and fear. Every day, I was constantly battling anxiety and nervous issues. I remember when I moved from London back to where my parents were in Rugby, and I could not even leave the house. I was so scared. The nerves were so bad that my mom kept saying to me, "Just walk to the end of the road, and come back. Just walk a little bit further down the road, and come back." It was very, very small steps—literally small steps that got me. It's still a battle for me, but I'm getting there.

Natalie was going through a rough time in her life, but she appreciated that it woke her up from a life she didn't necessarily want to live. She knew that the financial world wasn't going to make her happy. Although she was crippled with fear and anxiety, she appreciated her wake-up call.

Natalie became very aware of her situation. She was very aware that it was her fear that was holding her back from a *life most excellent*. She began to accept that she had to change. She couldn't go on living her life as it was, because it wasn't what she really wanted, and it wasn't making her feel fulfilled.

Natalie finally took accountability for what needed to change if she was going to live a life she was proud of. She made active steps toward what she really wanted. She knew that if she was going to achieve greatness, she needed to throw herself into whatever came next.

Natalie had been approached to host a Christian music show on satellite in the UK. At first, she was very hesitant. She knew that she had no experience in the field, and she didn't think she'd have too much to offer in terms of being a host. She eventually said no to the offer. But the producers kept insisting that she try it, and Natalie realized that it was just her fear standing in the way of her dreams. She realized it was a do-or-die situation, and that she was only going to overcome her fear if she leapt in head first; so she agreed to the offer. She said:

> *It's a case of "do-or-die" for me, because it's like, if I don't have a go at something, then life is empty for me. I may as well just take the courage to just step out, even if I feel like I'm going to pass out or I'm going to throw up if I have to speak in front of people. For me, it's just a case of, you know what? Just go and do it. It's like that; "feel the fear and do it anyway," and it's so true. You only overcome obstacles when you actually just "step out and do it" regardless of how you feel.*

When asked what her three best tips are for being a host, Natalie said: *do your research, really listen to the interviewee,* and *have confidence.* Natalie described an interview with someone who had recently written a book, and the interview had been arranged very quickly. She didn't have enough time to read the book, and the interview was very hard for her. Now, she always makes sure to get all the information she needs by researching beforehand.

When it comes to listening, she said, "When you're a host, it's not about you. You're there to share somebody else's story and somebody else's message. It's more about listening and not "I - I - I - me - me - me," and, "It's all about me," so really listen to what others are saying.

Confidence was her last piece of advice. She said, "Just have the confidence to believe that you can do it."

Natalie's most recent endeavor was in another area in which she had little to no experience: the film industry. Natalie never had a particular interest in film, but a recent connection she made prompted her to get involved with prescreening movies to discuss their meanings and messages with others. Recently, she prescreened a movie in the UK about the life of Nelson Mandela. This avenue of work allowed Natalie to be creative with her events. To illustrate Nelson Mandela's constant work towards reaching new goals, she created a Christmas tree in honor of him and had people write down and hang their goals for 2014 on the tree.

When asked about how Natalie manages her home life and raising a daughter with her work life, she said, "I believe there are seven key areas to living a balanced life: a time for work, health, relationships, community, personal development, spirituality, and 'me' time." She explained that making time for her family was essential to her, so she physically plans time on her calendar to do things with her family. It keeps things in order and balances her work life and home life.

When asked what general advice Natalie would share for women, she said simply, "It's all about action." Take Natalie's story, get inspired by her use of the five Foundational Pillars of a 24-Hour Woman, and make your own story happen.

Do you want to watch the full interview? Come on over to www. The24HourWoman.com/blog. Share with me your comments, and ask your questions. As always, I would love to hear from you.

Signpost for Chapter 8

It's time to take out your journal and get to massive action. Consider these questions as you reflect on Chapter 8:

1. What do you think are some habits you can cultivate that will help you thrive in work/business and life?
2. What are some mental strengths you can build and be focusing on?
3. Is your work/job allowing you to live the lifestyle you desire, which allows you to build towards your legacy? If not, what might the possible transition steps be?

Chapter 9

THE BIG OBSTACLE

"The Journey of a thousand miles begins with the first step."
–Lao Tzu

All women need to know that there are common, big roadblocks to success. And while there are endless solutions to overcoming them, we all have to find the unique pathways around the roadblocks that will work for our lives—including our families and careers. There is not a one-size-fits-all solution. While all of our journeys will be unique and personal, by learning from one another and examining case studies, we can absolutely learn how to navigate the real-life obstacles we'll come up against.

Let's talk about how to cross the line from planning to fruition—including some of the big roadblocks to success and how to overcome them. What are they, and how do we spot and work around them?

165

Where Do We Start? There's So Much to Do

One of the key pieces we realize, without fail, is that there's *so much to do*. This phenomenon is pervasive throughout the many phases and areas of our lives.

Yes, the to-do list can be a little overwhelming, but if we look at it as an opportunity, we will see there are some simple solutions. To begin with, we all have to start by addressing those obligations that are most important for us.

There's a great story that illustrates prioritizing away the overwhelm in life. It goes like this: A teacher stood before his class. He picked up a large, empty jar in front of him and began to fill it with rocks right to the top. He asked the students if the jar was full. They agreed it was. He then picked up a box of small pebbles, poured them into the jar, and shook it lightly. The pebbles rolled into the spaces between the rocks. He asked his students again if the jar was full. They agreed it was. He then picked up a bag of sand and poured it into the jar. He looked at the classroom of students, "I want you to recognize that this is your life. The rocks are the important things—your family, your partner, your health, and your children—anything so important to you that, if it were lost, you would be nearly destroyed. The pebbles are the other things in life that matter, but on a smaller scale—like your job, your house, or your car. The sand is everything else—the small stuff. If you put the sand or the pebbles into the jar first, there is no room for the rocks. The same goes for your life. If you spend all your energy and time on the small stuff, you will never have room for the things that are truly most important."

Here's the lesson: Pay attention to the things that are critical in your life. Define your TRUEST legacy. Take care of the most important things first—*the things that really matter*. Set your priorities.

You always have attention and time in the longer term for everything—but consider right now. What are the big pieces that you must do? Or what are the big pieces you must *have* in order to reach that most important legacy? Those things are NOT to be compromised. You must do them or put them in place. Period. And that means making choices.

Evaluating and prioritizing your life in terms of the big rocks and the sand might demand another round of clarity and discovery. The aim in this process is to refine your path even more so that it resembles exactly what are you trying to build at the end of the day—eliminating extraneous work that is unnecessary for your goals or legacy. Then, you will have overcome the first major roadblock: your overwhelmed feeling.

I Want This…This…This…and This…

The next roadblock you will be asked to conquer is this: When you make choices, there must be compromises. This may present a harsh reality that you have to face over and over in life as you choose what stays in and what goes out of your daily life. And it is one that involves balancing other people's needs and desires—such as those of your partner, children, parents, and friends.

What Have I Done? SOB

The third roadblock is *regret*. At any given moment, you can stand and look backward at what you've compromised and given up. You can feel very isolated in those moments, and that's why you need a community. That's why we have our online resources, because it's vital for you to feel that you are supported and that there will be others who will join you. There is no isolation. Other women have made the same sacrifices to move their lives and families forward, for generations.

Yes and YEs and YES

The fourth roadblock is the *ability (or inability) to say no*. We have had to sacrifice what we wanted many times in life before. Often we battle with how and when to say no, because we want to be liked *and* effective. We want to have vibrant and successful lives and legacies, and sometimes when saying no, we feel that we're being selfish. Actually, we are being selfish when we give in without contemplation and self-care, because we are depriving others of getting to know who we truly are.

People who know their legacy know, without a doubt, that they want a great action plan. But if they can't say no to people or things, they must re-examine how they manage the different areas of their lives.

If you must learn to say no, then that's a reset—and an important one.

You also may need to reset at different life stages by asking, *what are the new needs and demands on you and your life?* Always keep right in front of you a definition of your big picture in terms of the legacy that you want to leave behind. You live this life but once; that legacy is your lighthouse to guide you.

Five Considerations to Building Career Resilience

As you begin to lift the veil on your current job and position as a 24-Hour Woman, you may realize that the job you are working currently is not the one you will have for long. You may, in fact, realize that the job you have is about to be phased out of existence; or due to economic and business changes, your job/role might be affected. What you need most is to build your *career resilience*—which means that you are anticipating ways to thrive in a volatile, uncertain, complex, and ambiguous world. You are remaining engaged and bouncing back after setback.

How can you embed career resilience within your daily living? Rather than reacting to short-term change, the 24-Hour Woman creates long-term change by living mindfully through her career transitions. Here are five strategies:

1. **Develop a keen sense of awareness.**
   - What are three trends that might affect your industry? What are three trends that might affect your company's existence or performance? What are three trends that will affect your role? Knowing these gives you the leverage of preparing and broadening your options—turning changes into opportunities. Recall the era of mainframes evolving to the use of cloud computing? Keep your eye on developments. Be present, but future oriented.
   - Keep track of the knowledge, skills, and experience you possess that are mobile and portable.
   - What's your state of well-being? Remember, it's not just about wellness today. Invest in your health for the long haul, so that when the going gets tough, you march on.

2. **Be open to evolving your role/business as long as it builds towards your legacy.**
   - What are you most passionate about? Finding or carving out a role that is built upon your passion, and supported by your knowledge and skills in the context of the evolving reality, is key to building career resilience. This gives you the ability to leverage on your competence and ride on your confidence while remaining open to coaching and clarity about what you need to adapt.
   - Learn something new, and keep focused on growth.

3. **Get connected.**
   - Build your network and support before you need them. These could be networks within your company or industry. Look out for other groups of interest, like women entrepreneur networks or women in technology groups.
   - Identify and initiate mentoring relationships with those you wish to learn from or seek counsel from. Don't choose

just one person, but different people, each having traits that you value as you seek their counsel and guidance.

- Value-add and give to your network. Support one another. Invest in your social capital.
- Market yourself as a company of one.

4. **Look up.**
- Retain a huge dose of optimism and confidence despite whatever is happening. Do not let your state of well-being (or lack thereof) trip you on establishing your state of mind. Being future oriented is critical. This is another reason why you should develop growth friends; you can look to them for this encouragement. And ultimately, cultivate your belief that *the best is yet to be.*

5. **Develop the understanding that *you are a company of ONE.***
- Think like an entrepreneur. Until I became an entrepreneur, I did not fully understand what is needed to run a business and what it takes to make that business sustainable. Do you consider the work of your hands as a business? Then think like an entrepreneur, even if you are working within a company. You will see and act on unique opportunities, because you will think and act differently than an "employee."

•

Putting It Into Practice

How might you develop your career resilience muscle? Consider the example of Penny, who is a trained mechanical engineer.

- **Develop a keen sense of awareness.** She excelled in her area of work as an engineer, but realizing that the writing was on the wall as a female in an oil exploration company, she kept an eye on the developing trends where she could leverage her experience. She was willing to invest in her own learning and education.

- **Be open to evolving your role/business as long as it builds towards your legacy.** Penny was open to discontinuing her work as an engineer, but knew that her training as an engineer would stand her in good stead, as she was process driven, rational, and analytical.

- **Get connected.** Penny had wisely spent time once a fortnight to attend the Toastmasters program and events organized by her alumni. She reached out to her network as she wanted to transition to a different industry/role. As she had always been supportive of others, she received many e-connects and referrals to consider.

- **Look up**. She held fast to her belief that her future would be one of hope and brilliance. She did not give up or feel disillusionment.

- **Develop the understanding that *you are a company of ONE*.** From day one upon graduation, Penny had always considered her role as running a company of one. Whether she was making recommendations regarding a project, or in her supervisory role, she always considered that she was the owner of her unit; hence, she did not take things for granted. She stood out as a distinct employee, because she did not have an "entitled" mentality. When she left for her new role, she knew that she was merely transitioning to another business.

Building Career Resilience Is Like Building a Muscle

Yes, just as resilience is a muscle, so is career resilience. Exercising that muscle takes effort, but if you wait until something happens, you might end up losing the use of that muscle. You would then have to *re-gain* and *re-learn* the use of that muscle through painstaking physiotherapy. It costs much more time, money, and effort to *rebuild* resilience than it does to build it today.

What? My Beliefs?

Finally, the last obstacle that is huge for many is that people forget to reinforce their beliefs. They forget to remind themselves how important their legacies are, and therefore they get sucked into just endlessly running their to-do lists. They do not block out time, and certainly they do not move toward what they are looking to build, simply because they forget what they really value. Then, three, five, or ten years down the road, they will look back and say, *what wasted years.*

For example, we have a client in her thirties with two young children. She has a travelling job, but she felt that her job could be done remotely. When she looked at her legacy, she knew for sure that having a good marriage and raising two children to become contributors in the positive sense to the society around them held high importance for her.

She wanted to spend more time with them in their "growing up years," before they turned twelve. When we worked with her and determined her legacy, she said that in her heart, she deeply knew that those two kids were the real fruits of her life. This idea so strongly resonated with her that she began to cry, saying she would not give up. *A new path was in order.*

We helped her in terms of looking at her goal and determining the big pieces that needed to be put in place. Obviously, she needed finances, and she needed to keep her knowledge and skills covered. She needed to ensure that key relationships were maintained. She needed to make absolutely sure that, out of the seven areas of her life, she was implementing what needed to be put into place at her particular stage.

We worked with her to see how we could structure the job so she could create flexibility. She laughed and shared that nobody had ever asked for flexibility in her company. "If I ask, they will probably suggest for me to be fired." This fear definitely tested her belief around what she wanted from her life and in her legacy with her children. She decided *it was worth it to make a change.*

At the end of the day, she did her homework and approached her supervisor about gaining two days to work from home. To her pleasant surprise, her supervisor said, "Yes, why not? I see that most of the things you need to do can be consolidated. We'll evaluate, and you will have to demonstrate to me that you're contributing and doing a good job. In fact, you'll have to show that your derivative achievements can be done well, and that we all can work as an effective team."

First of all, it was a very pleasant surprise to her that she could start out with twenty-four hours a day on overwhelm—as a woman ready to hit burnout trying to meet everyone's needs including her own—and become a strong woman providing a solution. As a bonus, she potentially was paving the way for her teammates to take on alternate work setups.

Another example is Sylvia. You may remember that you met her in Chapter 1. She is below the age of thirty, works in an investment bank, and very often experiences no break in her day. She's new to the workplace, and has been told by everybody that "in the first few years of your career at the bank, there is no life. You just work."

When she chose to be in investment banking, she knew that she would have to work very long hours. But after a period of time, she asked herself the simple question, "Is it really worth it? Is this what I want my life to be known for?" The questions would continue... "What opportunities would I miss if I were to spend less time in my work? Am I really happy to pursue this other passion of mine—artistic endeavors—at all costs?" She was deeply torn whenever something happened around the holidays or with family. She would inevitably struggle with, "Can I take time off to do this?"

What she did was this: She examined her work time and began to look for job areas within her investment bank where the workload was a tad slower. Then, she took a chance to search for classes in those specific areas—to learn the skills she would need to make a shift within her company.

She tried to find ways to remain connected to her husband; doing so, to her, was as important as work. So they tried to share meals together. In relation to the seven areas of life, her choice to fit her husband into her day established a sense of renewal. It also fit into recreation, nourishment, and building relationships—all of which were important to her, beyond just work and career.

She began to look at the big pieces and the small pieces—and actually at her habits. She began to ask herself important questions. *What could she do every single day to add a little bit more value into her life—to find the small things that brighten a day?* The shift in her career could take time, so she looked at different ways to incorporate these other important facets into her life.

With technology, the iPhone became the tool for her to pursue her artistic interests with ease, because she could take pictures and start to make collages. She could use photos of pottery, and she could put them into visual art. So ultimately, she found a different way to enjoy her love for the arts, her renewal, and her creative expression, even though she was still holding onto a very demanding job. That shift in thinking and action brought her both peace and renewal. She was still very stressed, and very busy, but she also began to feel very fulfilled and happy.

In my own journey, every quarter, I reflect on my life. My actions have to revolve around what I really love. I do so much in my work, and it is all a creative expression of myself. It's easy for others to misunderstand.

Sometimes, family members come and say, "You're working harder than you used to when you were in the corporate world."

The initial idea when I started my own business was that I wanted to spend more time with my children. Now, I find creative ways that I can spend more time with them, sometimes by bringing them into the business; in that way, I bundle things together. When I go for a meeting where it is less formal, or with somebody who I've worked with or partnered with, for example, I bring my kids so that they "know what Mommy does."

Sometimes, when I do my video recordings, my second boy will be with me, helping with the lights. Then, we'll go for refreshments. I enjoy working with women, but I also enjoy my family and my boys. I want to be a big part of their lives. They're young now, but they will only be young once. As they grow up, yes, they may still want Mommy around, but the relationship will be different.

That has always been one the tensions and challenges in this twenty-four hour world: to find fulfillment and happiness between work and family and create some "ME" time. Work alone is not enough for renewal and sustainability, even if you love what you do. You need to unplug from work so that you get different perspectives and bring that value back to your career. That is one of my biggest realizations I've had about spending time for my own renewal without feeling guilty about blocking time for myself—whether it's with my family or husband or just by myself.

In fact, one of the reasons we recommend a strong community of other professionals at your level or in your genre—perhaps a mastermind group—is because it offers you time to unplug from the "business of business" and really become immersed with a like-minded group of people to learn, grow, and find strong support and friendships.

Another renewal step is to schedule time without technology—including cable and shows on demand, emails, computers, handheld games, and cell phones. Unplug. Disconnect. Get off the grid. Whatever you call it—create space and time that allows yourself time to think, reflect, and find a sense of appreciation and awareness.

This is one of the reasons I advocate journaling, because when you journal, you will not forget. As you journal throughout the year, you can step back and witness your benchmarks. You can see patterns and say, "Hey, that's when I made that choice, and that's why there's this difference right now." It serves as your own reference and navigation guide in your journey toward your legacy.

☆ ☆ ☆

"How I get through it: I am endlessly grateful."
—**Sallie Krawcheck** on what sustains her (Huffington, Arianna. LinkedIn Post, "Redefining Success: Takeaways from our Third Metric Conference." June 15, 2013.)

☆ ☆ ☆

Taking It Home: Five Great Holiday Tips
When You Travel With the Very Young/Elderly

I love the privilege of traveling with my parents and family, all at the same time. These "big group" tours are often done also with my sister and the family of one of my best friends, Elsie.

You can imagine what it's like to travel with a group of twelve to fourteen people—older folks along with the younger kids (at one time, the youngest was three and a half years old)! Elsie has mastered the skill of multigenerational travel. Lots of advance planning and coordination goes into this adventure. I call this "an adventure," because often we need to dose ourselves with a huge sense of humor.

Instead of being uptight with where we "should be" and what we "should have," we remind ourselves to enjoy the company. I always remember one saying, "Enjoy the present, as we never know what happens next."

These are some of my tips for arranging travel with elderly adults—including possibly your parents—and/or kids in tow. (You may also download the checklist and planning chart for this at www. The24HourWoman.com/Resources.)

1. **Determine a venue, city, or country that will offer diverse activities catering to the generations you travel with.** It's best to tour as a self-drive, or if the group is large enough, to have your own driver. Staying put in one place for a longer time will be easier than trying to cover a city in a day.

2. **Each day, map out something for each age group.** For example, schedule a trip to the aquarium in the morning, drive to a winery for the adults in the afternoon, and barbeque for all to chill out in the evening.

3. **Travel light.** You do not need the additional stress of keeping track of a lot of luggage. Pack wisely—and strategically, if you are going to places with extreme weather.

4. **Stay in apartments or accommodations with a kitchen where possible, especially when you travel with fairly young kids.** They may fancy a later morning breakfast before heading out. At the same time, this setup creates a more homey feeling. I like to use AirBAndB.com to make arrangements.

5. **If you have the means to cook or prepare meals, have at least one meal per day at "home."** This is less stressful than rushing through the process and hurrying everyone to be done just because breakfast is only served until 10 a.m. A vacation is meant for relaxing and enjoying one another's company!

What other tips or ideas do you have regarding traveling with older folks along with younger ones? I am sure my sister would have other thoughts to add! Email me at solutions@The24HourWoman.com. I would love to hear your ideas, and I am sure you will inspire and hopefully motivate others to take on the challenge of multi-generational travel.

The 24-Hour Woman Speaks
Ms. Mary Agnes Antonopoulos (US)
CEO and Founder, Viral Integrity

She didn't always possess her dream job. For more than twenty years, Mary Agnes worked as a secretary, and she excelled at her job. She used her skills as a writer to her advantage and was happy with her success in the workplace, but she knew she wanted more out of her career. Mary Agnes used the five Foundational Pillars to examine her goals in life and create her dream job and a *life most excellent.*

Mary Agnes had a profound *appreciation* for her job and the projects she was able to work on. She appreciated that she was not starting at ground zero; she had many skills that could transfer over to a number of different career paths.

Mary Agnes was very much *aware* of her position in life. She knew that something had to change for her to have the successful life she wanted. She was aware of the struggles that a career change might bring, but was also aware of how fast her life was going by. She knew that if she didn't act now, she might never get to where she wanted. Mary said: "I just knew that I was forty-one years old, and if I was ever going to go for my dream, time was passing. Time was passing every single day, and I wasn't going for it. It was long overdue by then." Mary Agnes understood what was holding her back and decided something needed to change.

She fully accepted that her position was going to change. She was going to abandon a career and lifestyle that she had become so accustomed to so that she could make her dream job a reality. To prepare for this transition, Mary Agnes stepped back and made a quick analysis of how she really wanted her life to look. She understood that a "start over" was a big decision. She asked herself, "If I were to start completely over in my career, what would I want to do?"

She said, "I decided to write. I had written my whole life. I started being a professional writer at fourteen. I was paid for my writing. I continued; in every job, in every company, I would write. In the mergers and acquisitions firms, I wrote their black books. In private equity, I redesigned everybody's files, as we brought in the new portfolio companies. Writing was a huge part of my career, and I decided to make it my only career."

After she made that plan, Mary Agnes took action. "I went into ghostwriting because, as a business woman, I really understood that writing a book for a year in hopes it might get published and in hopes of it making money was not going to work. I needed to make a living immediately, and I needed to be fruitful. I started ghostwriting. I had clients in the first ninety days. I was twenty thousand dollars positive year one, which isn't a fortune of money, but it was definitely a sign that I could do this for a living." Mary Agnes was able to leverage the skills she had to create a job that she was truly happy with.

Social media was the area where Mary Agnes's career really flourished. She learned the platforms, the algorithms, and the ins and outs of growing businesses using social media. She then took her writing skills and built her clients' online presences. When asked to share some of her greatest social media tips for business women, Mary Agnes said:

The LinkedIn profile is probably the most important thing we do online as professional women. There are lots of spaces for relationships and engagement, but the LinkedIn profile is almost like your online CV or your online resume. If it's not fully filled out, you're absolutely losing connections—probably business opportunities, even just relationships—because we know as women, the core of our successes come from the relationships we build. The most important thing that I think you can do on LinkedIn is to have a video. Video is very easily added, and it's hugely purposeful, because the best ambassador for you is actually you.

Mary Agnes then went on to explain that adding a PowerPoint to your LinkedIn profile can be a very powerful tool. Mary Agnes has many PowerPoints on LinkedIn that are easily accessible and downloadable for other women who do social media for a living, teach social media, or just want to use it in their companies to help their employees be more useful to the brand. Mary Agnes also suggests to showcase your strengths in your headline, not your title. She says, "My headline says 'ghostwriter, social media strategist, keynote speaker.' I have all of my assets in the headline, not my work history."

When asked to share some tips about how she balances home life with work life, specifically in terms of her daughter, Mary Agnes said that her biggest tip is to keep your promises. She said:

My company has really become very successful. I've really learned a lot from Cheryl, and I'm very grateful to get support around me, outsourcing tasks that I can outsource, and learning, really, when I make a promise, to keep my promises. If I say, "Darling, Mommy just needs ten more minutes, and then we'll go play cards," to put a timer and set that ten minutes, because ten minutes can easily become forty-five minutes, and then another call comes in from somebody else who needs me professionally. It doesn't happen. I've never been somebody who broke promises, and learning that one simple tactic from Cheryl has really been the love of my life, because I keep my promises, and my daughter knows she can count on me.

To balance her work life and home life, Mary Agnes has set boundaries in both areas. Not only does she set boundaries with regards to keeping her promises to her daughter, but also with her clients. She has realized that, with having so many clients, giving them full accessibility to her is unrealistic. She has learned to set better boundaries and create realistic expectations with them.

As a closing thought, Mary Agnes was asked to pinpoint the one great opportunity she sees right now and what women can do to seize it. Mary Agnes responded:

I think YouTube is a huge opportunity. As marketing for entrepreneurs develops, each elevation of brand builds your recognition. It builds your reputation. It builds your rapport. You are, like we said a little earlier, your best ambassador. I think the best opportunity is YouTube. Having a blog is very important, but it's very time-consuming. Google checks our websites to see if we're updating them regularly. One way to update your website regularly and easily is your blog, but how do you do that without investing two hours into writing this huge article that maybe nobody reads? I like YouTube videos. I do a two or three or four minute video. Then, I'll get it transcribed by one of the many transcription services. I'll fix the copy a little bit, and then I'll post it as a written blog.

When Mary Agnes's life wasn't going in the direction she was hoping for, she saw the opportunity to change it. She used the five Foundational Pillars of a 24-Hour Woman to leverage her skills and create the dream job and *life most excellent* that she had been seeking.

As you think about her story, I hope what she mentioned on leveraging social media also hits home as a way by which you may extend your influence, as it levels the playing field to reach the masses. Watch out for other platforms that level the playing field so you can thrive as a 24-Hour Woman.

Want to watch her full interview? Come on over to www. The24HourWoman.com/blog. Share with me your comments, and ask your questions. I would love to hear from you!

Signpost for Chapter 9

You've read how others have put the five Foundational Pillars into motion. Now, consider these questions as you reflect on Chapter 9 and how to put your learning into action:

1. In what way can you embed the five Foundational Pillars into your day-to-day living, demonstrating them in the seven areas of your life?
2. What major mind "blocks" do you need to overcome?
3. How can you bring joy and presence into your journey?

Chapter 10

MARCHING ORDERS

"We each have twenty-four hours.
How will you spend yours wisely?"
—Cheryl Liew-Chng

*E*sther has learned the secrets of the 24-Hour Woman. Today, she knows how her life's daily weaving (daily investments of her time and energy, putting all she learned in action) reveal a beautiful tapestry. This is her life's legacy.

First of all, she realized what she got into initially was not the legacy that she had planned or hoped for. She sat down with us, and we worked through that issue FIRST. As she began the discussion, she realized that her legacy wasn't just about her career and professional aspirations, but about relationships—particularly with her children and husband. The real value she held dearly was the relationship with her children; this was the major part of the legacy that she wanted to leave behind. So adjustments had to be made.

We asked her to explore, from a daily basis and a big thesis basis, *"What do you need to be doing in the seven areas of your life?"* Relationships were a big piece that she was working through—because she was not about to give them up. She really loved what she was doing with her health and the different pieces of her professional life, but there were adjustments needed. As she looked at these factors, she said, "Okay, these are a priority for me right now, because Matthew is so young."

From there, she began to build and identify, "These are the pieces I need to look at. Let's start with the first Pillar of *appreciation*. What can I appreciate now in terms of my health? How do I appreciate my relationships so I can build my support base? What can I be doing in terms of my community involvement? What can I appreciate?" She began to realize that her neighbors were playing a huge part, because on days when she was not available, the neighbors were the ones who chipped in to ferry Matt to and from class or to watch over him while both she and her husband were at work.

She began to look at her life from a position of the seven areas and stepped back to see what was going on and reflect, "Hey, it's not that bad. I have some pieces in place that already are working for me." This also created a heightened sense of awareness as she worked through things.

For yourself, rating from 1 to 10, where do you think you are now in terms of how you want to feel about your career? How about your family relationships? Where do you think this rating should be, and why? Is it aligned to the legacy that you want? This exploration work goes back to the fundamentals that align to form your legacy. **Is there congruence between your actions today and the legacy you want to lead? Does what you are doing today make sense, and is it able to unfold accordingly to help you achieve vibrancy?**

For our client, as she built from her plan, she realized that her job was not tearing her away from the legacy she wanted to leave behind. She realized that her current job had certain rules and perceived restrictions. Having said that, she loved her job, and decided she would like to see how she could make things different.

She began to look at more creative ways of getting the same role done in a different manner, working a little bit harder with the same exposure, instead of being relocated overseas for an entire twelve to eighteen months. After thinking and working through different options, she spoke with her supervisor. She walked him through a very comprehensive plan that addressed what she valued (including being a part of his team), where she was in her career, and what she hoped to accomplish. But she also expressed to him that there were other things happening in her life, and she needed to come up with a plan that would allow her to contribute both to his team, as well as to her own goals.

She laid it out to him and said, "What if we just test this out for six months, and see how it unfolds—assessing the outcome and how the team works with it?" She didn't say, "Oh, Boss! I have a problem..." She went in with solutions.

She took accountability. She knew that if her plan could be successful, it would help her build something—sewing another thread instead of putting a tear into the tapestry of her legacy.

Her supervisor was a little bit hesitant, because they had not "done this sort of thing before," particularly with someone of high potential. They had a very strict rule that those in her role had to go for an overseas assignment for twelve to eighteen months if they wanted to grow in their careers. High potential people were expected to be prepared for this. It did seem as if she was rocking the boat for someone who was trying to achieve a more senior position. The supervisor was open to give it a try, but laid out the cards to say, "If this does not take flight, other things might be in jeopardy."

In terms of her exposure, she was able to negotiate much less time away from her family, rather than twelve months at a time. It took time to convince everyone that her plan could work, but at the end of the day, the result was *awesome*. For Esther, it was worth it to advocate for this change, because she felt that she was activating her own creativity, sense of control, and collaboration. She was moving toward what she wanted to do in order to be authentically herself—with her supervisor and her team.

Esther worked through the six months as a pilot. The new system worked well for Esther and her team. The team felt more important and became more collaborative.

Today, Esther still has distance to travel in optimizing her work setup, despite making progress. She hasn't yet felt the full impact she needs, and she hasn't gotten her teeth into the meatiest of the part of the exposure, but she is feeling much more satisfied. "I'm knowing it and getting something out of it. It might take a bit longer for me to get to a leadership position, but counting the cost it takes for my family to take the traditional route to getting there, I'm not willing to pay that price." She has created a win between home and her workplace. Most of all, Daniel, her husband, has felt that she has been taking a more proactive role in being a mom, being available, and being involved in the family and household.

All around, Esther is still a work in progress, because she's in a life stage right now where Matt is still young. As she progresses in her career, and as Matt grows up, she will continually need to refine her legacy and assess the seven areas in her life; but the five Pillars will give her a strong foundation.

Remember, your life and your legacy are not cast in stone. It is never too late to look at what you are building and determine if it's propelling you towards your own legacy. If you look again, you may start to realize the real question in your own life: "What's the legacy I want to leave behind?"

For Esther, it was also, "Oh gosh! I'm in my fifties; do I have time?" Yes, *she has time.*

It doesn't matter when you start, as long as you start and construct the building blocks. You are closer to where you want your legacy to be than when you started. Wherever you are right now, whatever life issues you are encountering, *now is always a great time to start.*

Five Factors to Consider in Starting Your Own Business

A common progression from feeling a lack of autonomy at work, or feeling a misalignment between work and personal life, is for women to jump onto the entrepreneurial bandwagon. If you think, "Oh great. I will be my own boss, and all will be simple!", think again. Consider that all issues, big or small, eventually end with you. You hire your team members (as full-time staff or on a freelance basis), or you are the "one woman shop." Time is your own only if you set boundaries and expectations of engagement with your clients and suppliers.

When I first started to think about starting my own business, I was most inspired by a book called *Joyfully Jobless,* by Barbara Winter. It helped me realize that what was key for me was the joy that the business brings. Here's what else I considered as I interviewed and joined mastermind sessions with other entrepreneurs who were addressing some of the basic considerations:

1. **Ask yourself, "What is the goal of starting the business?"** This helps to ensure that the business is designed according to your legacy and not creating someone else's. What's your passion? You get to chose what to create.

2. **Consider the product or service that you will provide.** It should support your desired lifestyle. What do you want to build?

3. **Consider all of your options.** How about creating multiple profit centers? You can start with one area and then add other complementing offers to your audience over time.

4. **Don't let your small business make you think small.** That's something that I have heard over and over again. I agree with this philosophy. All of the big names we hear about all started as small businesses. But you decide how large it will be. *Small Giants,* by Bo Burlingham, provides a different perspective of measuring success besides growing large.

5. **Consider the different aspects of the business.** Marketing on a shoestring to start, as many entrepreneurs must do, means that you need to be clear about who you serve. What's the avatar or profile of your most satisfied client? You also need to manage your cash flow. For me, the greatest learning was to manage cash flow to ensure that I had a reserve of least twelve months of cash for expenses to help myself get to a place of profitability, transition to a new business model or undergo a reinvention, or manage any potential downturns I may experience—such as with the economy. It's natural for a business to experience ebbs and flows, and as an entrepreneur, you need to be prepared to pull through them. The last thing you need is the additional stress of financing your business in the short-term as you are building for the long-term; build up a reserve so that you don't have this worry. Also, do your best to ensure that you manage your suppliers in the most collaborative manner.

There is a lot to consider for those who launch and scale up their businesses. Come over to www.The24HourWoman.com/Resources for more inspiration and instructions.

Putting It Into Practice

Here's the journey of Jamie, who I coached. Jaime was working while raising two toddlers with her husband in Shanghai. She started toying with the idea of starting a business, because she had experienced enough of leaving her children crying at the door whenever she traveled. She loved interacting with and helping others. So she thought she would do something along the lines of helping women in transitions—just like she would need if she decided to leave the corporate life to discover her next endeavor.

- **Ask yourself, "What is the goal of starting the business?"** Jamie asked herself to define her purpose in starting a business. She considered her legacy. She knew that achieving it would take an investment of her time and effort. She concluded that she wanted to have an income and yet be able to raise her family. She did not want to travel if it meant staying overnight in hotels. She would rather set up in the morning and be back in the evening— in time for dinner with her family.
- **Consider the product or service that you will provide.** Based on her desire to serve others through helping, like she did as a supervisor in her corporate role, she started a coaching practice targeting the professional and stay-home moms who she met daily when she dropped of

her children for classes. They became her prospects, and because they met often and spent cumulative time together, she was able to ascertain a certain level of trust and likability. She held a luncheon for forty of these women, and ten later came forward and paid for her service. This allowed her to meet and work with them while meeting her household needs.

- **Consider all of your options.** Starting with one area, and then adding other complementing offers to her audience, Jamie started a monthly newsletter for those who were not enrolled in her services. Over time, more had opted into her newsletter. These people eventually became her audience for her paid webinars and other offerings. She had multiple offerings/profit centers that allowed her to live the lifestyle she desired as she built her legacy.

- **Don't let your small business make you think small.** Jamie started in Shanghai, but over time, through word of mouth, she had people wanting to attend her coaching sessions from Beijing, Guangzhou, Tianjin, and other cities. She realized that the potential of her business wasn't limited by her decision to stay home; her market and business could extend beyond Shanghai.

- **Consider the different aspects of the business.** Jamie started with just one coaching group and built her resources from the ground up, one step at a time. It would have been great if she'd had a traditional business plan; but then again, she might never have started the business, as the cost of business in Shanghai is very high. Most traditional business plans include securing an office space or "shop front" outside of the home, for example, which is expensive. But her coaching plan did not require much start-up capital. She was able to start small—managing her costs as she evolved—rather than having a business plan with numbers that might have frightened her off from starting.

I want to share one final, but important, thought as you move ahead: *feel the fear and anxiety, but do it anyway*. Being an entrepreneur without the safety net of the corporate structure and resources has to be the greatest personal development program in existence. You may not have all of the answers today, but through asking the right questions and activating the Five Pillars, you have every opportunity to succeed. You will acquire what you need as you grow—as long as you focus continually on your legacy.

Many of us have been running around in circles or on the treadmill for such a long time that we are just on autopilot. We are steered based on what society tells us and what was told to us as we were growing up.

The truth of the matter is, there is nothing new that's being presented as groundbreaking. We simply package and present things in new ways. Certainly, the fundamental longing or questions that we all have in the backs of our heads stay the same: "What am I here for?" "What is my purpose?" "Why am I doing all of this?" Those fundamental pieces—surrounding our *ultimate purpose*—is what all human beings search for. We want to feel a sense of connectedness to that purpose.

We have interviewed individuals who were multimillionaires, yet, if you ask them, finances were but a means to a purpose. The money itself didn't create a *life most excellent*. The ONLY meaning in money came through what it might have brought them in terms of fulfilling their legacies.

There's a drive towards purpose—a purpose of why am I here, a purpose of who do I want to be. That leads either to reflecting the journey that you're on as you are building, or it reflects the legacy that you want to be leaving behind. It's only through realizing the answer to *what's my purpose?* that your passion and presence will take form, because without knowing your purpose, there is no enthusiasm, and when there's no enthusiasm, there's no need to be present.

You can be at a certain meeting or session and perform, yet be totally switched off. Finding the purpose of what you want to be, and then reflecting why your legacy is defined in that manner, is crucial. How do you define your legacy? Is it as a mother? Something else? Now is the time to decide, so that you can begin living more intentionally and vibrantly.

Always dig deeper. When I ask you, *"What is your legacy?"* if you were to say, "My legacy is my relationship with X, Y, Z," then, I will dig deeper and ask, *"Why?"*

The emotion behind so much of what defines our legacy is love. *What do you care about? What drives you to be present? How can you begin to activate the five Pillars that will help you in getting the seven areas of life in order, such that you are consistently looking at hitting that greater purpose every single day?*

Finding your passion, choosing your focus, prioritizing where you are in your life, and having peace with your decisions is not easy. It's important to remember that they are NOT cast in stone, and you may have to shift and adjust throughout life several times, for a variety of great reasons—like supporting an elderly parent or heading back to school for a newly available certification.

This book has gifted you with the Foundational Pillars; now, take time to journal and gain clarity on your legacy. This is critical. In your day-to-day, remember that consistent discipline—and conscious designing, awareness, and ownership in terms of your choices—will build the tenacity and the inner strength you'll need to maneuver when the storms brew. When life shows up, you will be able to stay the course and weave the legacy YOU define and design.

Be bold, and take courage, because it is often the roadblocks in life that help us become the best women we can be. Like a sculptor working with the flaws in a beautiful piece of marble, these storms carve away the parts of ourselves that are not authentic to our legacies. They refine us.

THIS is a life that's most excellent, one that's joyful and vibrant. And it can start now, wherever you are in your journey.

Here's the ultimate question for all of us: We each have twenty-four hours. How will you spend yours? Invest in what matters most. And invest the TIME to *decide* what matters most. That is what Esther did to create a *life most excellent*. Now it's your turn.

"May you live all the days of your life."
–Jonathan Swift

Taking It Home: Five Things to Prepare Before Going on Business Trips

As roles and business becomes more global, even when leveraging on technology, there will be occasions when you will need to travel for meetings, conferences, or events. I know these challenges both from my corporate job and now as an entrepreneur. Even now that I work in my own business, I still need to travel—during some seasons more often than others.

As such, I have developed some standard procedures that I trust you will find useful. **Here are my five key considerations**: (You may also download the checklist and planning chart for this at www. The24HourWoman.com/Resources.)

1. **Communication**
   - **Love Expressed.** I tend to have little communication pieces for my family members—sometimes my parents, spouse, sister, and certainly for my boys. I stash notes in my sons' soccer training bags, send postcards, and occasionally leave notes pinned to the all-in-one calendar on the refrigerator. Many of my students have since instituted their own communication gestures, and thus have found great ways to reinforce their relationships even when they are away.
   - **Important and Urgent.** Contacts that are critical for the period I am away, or contacts for emergencies, are pinned to the calendar, once again for quick reference.

2. **Schedules**
   - **Calendar.** To avoid disruptions that needed to be managed while away, schedules for everyone involved with the family are all consolidated into one large calendar. This also makes it easy for caregivers to check what's happening when and who is involved. This has saved the day often in my household and eliminated the need for me to receive and answer small questions via text or overseas calls. Prior to travel, this also allows me to counter-check with my husband on his schedule so that one of us is always at home with the children.

3. **Meal Plans**
   - **Planning Ahead.** Providing my family with good, nutritious meals is my means of expressing love and concern. Depending on how long I will be away, I prepare ahead the meal plan for breakfast and dinner. Some of

my students have modified this method by having family members co-design their meal plans together. That way, there is ownership and "eat-ability" even when they are away.

4. **Keeping in Touch**
   - **Leverage Technology.** This is where I love technology. Using Google Hangouts, Skype, and FaceTime, I am able to keep in touch with my family even while away. So my number one most important criteria in choice of accommodation, besides safety, is naturally a good WiFi connection.

5. **Packing Convenience**
   - **Clothing.** I tend to travel as light as possible in terms of putting a wardrobe together. I typically pack: a three-piece suit (jacket, skirt, and trousers in a matching set, usually in light wool), a dress for the evening (in a classic red or black), and two cardigan sets in cotton or cashmere depending on the season (one in color and the other in cream or black). A colored/textured shawl is a must for travel on flights or to keep out the evening chill. I also never leave home without my workout track shoes, three-inch heels, and a higher one for events or night wear. The rest of my packing involves just throwing in my travel tee shirt and shorts, PJs, etc.
   - **Documents.** All of my documents are kept in plastic files, and travel documents are kept in Ziploc bags. On the plane, I carry on my main documents and notebook with external hard-disks, a light sweater/shawl, change of meeting wear, and walking shoes. I learned this after I had a bad experience years ago, when I arrived at my destination, and my checked-in baggage did not arrive. I needed to get to a meeting shortly upon arrival.

What other tips or ideas do you have for being effective and efficient in your dual roles—even as your job/business requires you to travel? Email me at solutions@The24HourWoman.com I would love to hear your ideas, and I am sure you will inspire and encourage others.

24-Hour Woman Speaks

Anne Samoilov (US)
Founder, AnneSamoilov.com

Anne Samoilov teaches solopreneurs how to be more productive—and create and launch their life's work in the form of products. She offers them not only the expertise to guide them through the process—but also the courage.

For Anne, landing in her current role was as natural as being born. Anne explains her journey like this: "I kind of feel like I did just end up here...I've been producing—which is kind of like launching—since the womb. I came out, and I was putting together shows and things when I was a child, so it does not surprise me now to look back at all of that and see what has happened."

Anne started her journey in film school, which she explains as "managing a bunch of pieces, being a director, putting things together," before she moved into working with visual effects and animation. Of that position, she says,

It was just an entry-level job. I didn't really know that it was exactly right. I just took a job because I knew some people who worked there, and it was at a really great company with Steven Spielberg. That part of it excited me. I thought, "Okay, exciting ideas, exciting stuff, I don't know where I'm going to fit in here eventually, but this could work...This is a really cool company, they're doing really interesting things, there are a lot of really creative people here." I got to be an onlooker, an observer of the creation, but not really one of the creators. I never felt prepared for it, ever. My husband is an animator, so he is on the other side of the fence from me. We met at one of the companies, but I always felt like I was such a fraud because I jumped in, was just kind of figuring it out, just felt out what the process was. I didn't know everything, but I was able to survive and still help things get out the door, still help ship things.

In the midst of surviving and learning, Anne built her credibility by nurturing the people on her team. She advocated for them with leaders, instead of just passing along messages. "I was always standing up for them...I was also working side by side with them. I was not just a manager who handed out work and then left."

In visual effects, the work often required long hours, and so that meant Anne often had to work overnights. "I was just there with the team, 'let's do this.'" She added, "I think that's kind of what I do now. I like to make sure I'm there and make sure people don't feel alone."

Today, Anne's team is distributed, as her organization has spread virtually. While she works alone much of the time, she has developed strategies for managing her virtual teams, which are useful to consider as we see trends moving towards more teams being managed virtually:

It's important to know that there are going to be people who are very communicative to you. They are going to tell you everything they are doing. You aren't going to have to worry about them; you're going to hand off work and they are going to do it. There are going to be other people who will still do their work, but they won't tell you what they're doing, and that's the hard part. If you are on a team, in an office, you can just jump over and be like, "Hey, everything okay?" Whereas if you keep sending someone emails like that, it's kind of weird. You just have to build in very regular communication, like daily huddles. Make sure there is a system in place, so there are normal, regular meetings. Then, it's not like you are micromanaging. If you are working in a physical space, people don't feel micromanaged if you pass by their office and say, "Hey, how's it going?" But in a virtual environment, you can't keep checking in on someone, or that's exactly how it feels.

Anne advocates communicating with everyone on the team about the larger context of what is going on, and who is doing what. She asks team members to repeat back what they are working on, so that everyone is clear.

Certain things you take for granted in a physical environment just are gone in this virtual environment. If you worked with someone like a web developer, they have been working for months and then they just disappear. What can you do? If someone gets hurt, sick, or worse, you're like, "oh, I'm done." It is difficult, but it's also rewarding when you have those systems in place, you have a Hangout once a week, you have Skype calls throughout the week, or you do daily huddles in different environments.

In the couple of years Anne spent in the corporate setting, the skill she feels that she transferred to her own business and leveraged is the *knowledge of how systems actually help a business.* "I know it's easy to work in a corporate environment and think that the systems are not allowing you to get your work done. It's very bureaucratic, all these things, but the systems actually do set you free on some level," Anne says.

She also learned how to pay attention to the financial side of the business—how things are set up and how employees and team members are hired and paid. "Systems are key," she said. "My project management background has been good, because it has allowed me to break everything down into those tasks, and to get things done."

Anne has found special ways to manage work-life as a 24-Hour Woman.

When I first decided to go completely, 100 percent independent, I actually got some co-working space, because I thought I should work in an office somewhat a few days a week just to make sure I stayed regimented. It actually hurt my productivity. Now I try to bust through as much work as I can at the beginning of the day, because I know things go downhill after that...I have a specific time I have to go help my daughter's class. I volunteer in my daughter's classroom in the afternoons, one day a week. There are other things that happen at the school, too, that I am there for, and so it's really not much time; she's there from 9 a.m. to 2 p.m. If I'm not wrapping stuff up by 2 p.m., it's bad all around.

The time constraints help her push through to be more productive. In fact, she explains that when her daughter is home sick with her, she often gets more done, because she has to be very focused. The mental framing helps.

Anne went on to talk about how she fits in ME time: "I have to force myself to get out of the house. I am not very good at balancing things. Even at night when I should be relaxing, maybe watching a movie, talking to my husband, eating a nice dinner, I often am like, 'I'm not working!'" She has had to create systems to ensure that she takes adequate time to nurture her home and personal life.

When Anne helps entrepreneurs launch their products and businesses, the first thing she asks them is, "Who are you doing this for?" People are key, she believes—whether in a corporate job or when launching a business.

> *It doesn't matter how cool your idea is...It's about looking and finding out what people need and giving that to them in a way that supports your passions as well. But it's not about trying to give something they don't want. I always start with the customer, the who it's for, and then from there it's just a matter of finding out if they have already talked to that person, are they putting out normal communication to that person. This part usually takes the longest to establish, that regular communication, getting to know who those people are and just drumming that in, what you do for those people.*

If Anne were to give advice to those starting their careers today, she says to take the job you are applying for and make it your own. "After you prove yourself in one area, you have much more leverage... Once you get to the point where you really are someone who is thought of as somewhat indispensable...you have some major leverage in the company." Then, she says, "You can start deciding, *what do I want this work to be?*"

If you want to watch the full interview, visit www.The24HourWoman. com/blog. Share your comments and questions. I would love to hear from you!

Signpost for Chapter 10

There are so many stories and case studies for you to consider.

It's time to ponder the bigger picture, now that you have reached the final chapter.

"I know for sure that what we dwell on is who we become."
–Oprah Winfrey

1. Imagine and create mental pictures of how you want to *live* every single day. I mean truly live—with vibrancy, with joy, and in fulfillment. You may journal, compose a song, create a collage of pictures, or draw. From the time you awake until you rest, dream about what your life could like. Block-out time, and creatively express how you want to *live* every single day.

2. Share your vision with one other person or a group who would truly support you as a 24-Hour Woman. Begin to *live authentically* each day!

CLOSING WORDS

"May the road rise up to meet you.
May the wind be always at your back.
May the sun shine warm upon your face;
the rains fall soft upon your fields and until we meet again,
may God hold you in the palm of His hand."
—Traditional Gaelic blessing

The time is now. The 24-Hour Woman who is stressed, overwhelmed, and struggling to achieve fulfillment can *have it all*—defined truly by her own authentic self. I am so excited and enthused about your future. Your conversations will shift from those of negativity and complaining to those of gratitude and appreciation. You no longer need to fear how to manage the dual role of work/business with your personal life. Instead, you can thrive and love life. You can be one who acknowledges the past and present but looks upon the future—full of hope and taking action. Through it all, you can engage in great celebrations as a 24-Hour Woman who thrives in life. I look forward to hearing from you.

As I write this book and review the materials myself, I am once again recharged. As we conclude, I want to leave you with the three steps I would suggest you get started with today. If you do nothing else, simply follow these three guidelines so that you can begin laying a foundation towards achieving your lifelong legacy—and earning your place as a 24-Hour Woman:

1. **Identify three ways you will keep your "why" and focus on your long-term legacy.**
2. **Identify your core supporters and cheerleaders, and enlist them.**
3. **Identify what you can do this week to strengthen the five Foundational Pillars in the different priority areas of your life. <u>Those Pillars again are:</u>**
   - **Appreciation,**
   - **Awareness,**
   - **Acceptance,**
   - **Accountability, and**
   - **Action.**

Remember to re-visit and refine your legacy statements—and refine your alignment in the seven priority areas—monthly.

You can do it. There are already elements in these five Pillars working for you. You have had the experience of success, no matter how large or small, in all seven different areas of your life, in your different roles as a 24-Hour Woman. The stories of the women in this book have shed light on ways to optimize your life. www.The24HourWoman.com has resources to support you, and I am here to journey with you as your guide and companion. You will see that no two stories of the 24-Hour

Woman are the same, but the tapestry of each is just as rich. Yours, too, will become that of a 24-Hour Woman who is living out her legacy to experience a *life most excellent.* I can't wait to hear from you.

STAY CONNECTED
WITH CHERYL

Connect with Cheryl through these platforms, and receive valuable resources that will inspire and empower you to thrive in work/business and life.

The24HourWoman.com
Facebook.com/24HourWoman
Youtube.com/The24HourWoman
www.Linkedin.com/in/cherylliewchng
Twitter/The24HourWoman

For corporate clients, please refer to
www.LifeWorkz.asia

ACKNOWLEDGMENTS

I am so greatly blessed, highly favored, and deeply loved by my Daddy God. I am so thankful for His wisdom and grace. The path I have walked, the different facets of my journey as a 24-Hour Woman, and the overall experiences I have gained have allowed me to express myself creatively in this book and in my life. *Thank you, Daddy God.*

This book is dedicated to my parents, who have loved and supported me in any way I've needed. Thank you, Ma and Pa.

To my beloved husband, who stood by me in all of the madness of my different career transitions and business challenges while raising our boys—Eng How, thank you, *My Dearest.*

To my sister, Pearlyn, you have been my supporter since we were young, and you continue to be in my corner. Your kind thoughts, gestures, and prayers have been so vital to me.

To Elsie Szto, Jacqueline Pang, and Teresa Chee—my growth friends who challenge me, support me, and have grown with me since our graduation—thank you; your lifelong, deep friendships are a rare gift.

To the 24-Hour Women who I have been blessed to learn much from at close proximity: Dr. Jennifer Lee (what a wonderful role model), Mrs. Jessie Phua (you showed me what clear-mindedness and tenacity can bring), Dr. Carolyn Tan (you showed me that transitions are possible, no matter how great, and that the gratitude and appreciation that one expresses are a measure of that inner person).

To the many colleagues I had in KK Women's and Children's Hospital where I spent almost ten years of my work-life, thank you. I learned so much from you about managing generations at work, work-life flexibility, building credibility, working together as a diverse team for our patients, and the choices each one of us makes towards building our legacies.

To Brendon Burchard, my mentor, teacher, coach and a trailblazer, thank you for taking your message so seriously and sharing it with such joy.

To my dear friend, Laura Steward, who nudged me to pitch my idea for the book to the publishers—not once, not twice, but three times before I felt that it was the "right time." Thank you, Laura, and Terry Whalen (Morgan James Publishing), the acquisitions editor, for believing in me.

To the team at Morgan James Publishing—David Hancock, Rick Frishman, W. Terry Whalin, Nickcole Wakins, Tiffany Gibson and Bethany Marshall—thank you for making it possible to put this out there.

To Jocelyn Godfrey of Spiritus Communications, my editor, I can't imagine how I could have ever gotten this done without you. Your questions, thoughts, and comments have refined the manuscript to serve all who read the book.

To Mary Agnes Antonopoulos of Viral Integrity, my dear friend who helped me articulate the various parts of the book and go through the transcriptions, thank you.

To the women whose stories were told in the book, I am grateful to you for the opportunity to demonstrate through you that it is possible for the 24-Hour Woman to thrive and live a vibrant life while building her legacy.

To the amazing people who have become my friends through the various Brendon Burchard events, particularly members of the Centre Ring Family—Cheryl Bonini Ellis, Dr. Susanne Bennett, Lori Barr, Carlos Marin, Mark Garcia, Gry Sinding, Wolfgang Payne, Nikki Nitz, Camper Bull, Jose Gomez, Jefferson Santos, Natalie Brown, Micki Aronson, Wayne Pernell, Lisa Scholnick, Allan Ting, Alan Christianson, Mikell Parsons and JJ Virgin—I learned so much from all of you in the pursuit of sharing your messages.

To the senior pastor of New Creation Church in Singapore, Pastor Joseph Prince, for sharing the gospel of grace, my source—and the NCC care group—thank you.

It's not possible to thank everyone who has helped me in my journey and process of creating The 24-Hour Woman message to launch a movement towards *living a vibrant, joyful life that builds towards a legacy*; I do apologize to all of my supporters, affiliates, fans, and friends who I have not listed here. I appreciate you and thank you for being a part of my journey.

To all of the women who I have worked with and will work with in the future to design *a life that is vibrant, joyful, and fulfilling*, this is your time to make that shift and *thrive*.

To all: *you matter; invest in what matters most.*

ABOUT THE AUTHOR

Cheryl Liew-Chng is the CEO and Founder of LifeWorkz Pte. Ltd., an Asian-grown firm that partners globally with organizations to create inspiring workplaces where talent thrives. As an inspiring leader and coach, Cheryl has helped leaders and organizations more effectively create excellent, contemporary workplaces that optimize their talent pools against a complex and volatile marketplace.

Cheryl's work in creating contemporary workplaces; leveraging workplace flexibility; and fostering culture, gender, and generational diversity have made her an in-demand and innovative expert in the business and government sectors.

She believes that individuals can live "lives most excellent" based on their own definitions of success. She guides these individuals—who come to know who they are and how they can contribute—in experiencing the joys and vibrancy of life. As a result, these individuals shape the future of work and of their communities.

An inspiring, in-demand speaker, trainer, and coach, Cheryl has helped thousands of individuals across the globe more consciously and effectively re-design their lives to discover delight in all areas—family, work, and play—so that they can find joy in giving and receiving the very best.

Cheryl's work inspires and empowers women globally. Starting in the workplace, her "StepUp for Women"™ and "The 24-Hour Woman" programs (online training and live events for personal and professional development) have impacted women professionals, stay-at-home moms, and entrepreneurs to be effective in both their current roles and the advancement of their careers or businesses. Her clients have included government agencies and dozens of private sector partners including multinationals with global presences. Her work was recognized by the World HRD Congress who presented her with the Global HR Excellence Award.

Cheryl is a working mom who, together with her husband, raises their three boys.

Cheryl's events include "Impact and Influence: The 24-Hour Woman Live," "StepUp for Women Live," and "High Performance Breakthroughs". Meet Cheryl and receive free training at www. The24HourWoman.com. Or for corporate clients wanting to evolve a contemporary organization, meet Cheryl at www.LifeWorkz.asia.

PROGRAMS BY CHERYL LIEW-CHNG

"The 24-Hour Woman™"

"StepUp for Women"

"Navigating Work-Life"

"High Performance Breakthroughs"

Meet Cheryl online and receive free training at
www.The24HourWoman.com